WILTON
GIFTS
from the
KITCHEN

Recipes and Ideas
for Take-Along Gifts

IN THESE BUSY TIMES, a gift of homemade food is more meaningful than ever. Bringing a treat from your kitchen along when you pay a visit to friends is a wonderful, personal way to thank your hostess. Sending a signature dessert to loved ones far away ensures they'll be thinking and talking about your thoughtfulness for days to come.

Gifts From The Kitchen can help you select just the right recipe to give. There is something here for every occasion, and for those times when you don't need a reason to give something special. You'll find delicious appetizers, entrees and desserts to please every taste and any lifestyle – from low-sugar cookies and a heart-healthy canapé to sinfully rich chocolate cakes...from an ideal meal for those starting in a new apartment (including the cooking tools they'll need in the future) to a fast and filling sandwich break for friends on moving day. Holiday ideas, treats for kids to make and give, picnic and tailgate lunches – even special snacks for animals... *Gifts From The Kitchen* has it all.

Best of all, these luscious foods are made to be easily transported or shipped. On every page, we'll show you pretty and practical ways to package your gift after cooking. We've even included a special section with suggestions for wrapping and sending foods, so they arrive looking as great as when they left your kitchen.

For those who love to share and receive the gift of food, *Gifts From The Kitchen* is the perfect surprise package.

PART I

ANYTIME GIFTS

*You don't have to be celebrating a holiday
or special occasion to give a gift from
your kitchen. That's why we call these
"Anytime Gifts." Whether you need a hostess
gift, a dessert for new neighbors, or a
different make-and-take dish for the office
potluck, we have delicious recipes, easy serving
suggestions, and creative packaging ideas for you.*

When new folks move into the neighborhood, welcome them with warm hospitality and a homemade dessert. This is a deluxe variation of America's number one favorite pie—APPLE. It features a cinnamon and brandy flavored apple-raisin filling and a streusel topping with walnuts and almond brickle bits. Bake it in Wilton's Pie Pan with Drip Rim—a wide rimmed pan that prevents messy spillovers in your oven. An apple pastry garnish is simple to make with Wilton's Apple Cookie Cutter.

Apple Streusel Pie

Wilton 9-in. Pie Pan with
   Drip Rim
Wilton Apple Perimeter
   Cookie Cutter

Pastry Crust:
1½ cups flour
½ teaspoon salt
¼ cup butter
¼ cup shortening
½ cup (2 oz.) grated mild natural
   cheddar cheese (optional)
2-3 tablespoons cold water

Filling:
¼ cup butter
8-10 Granny Smith apples,
   peeled, sliced
½ cup dark raisins or dried
   cranberries
½ cup packed brown sugar
¼ cup granulated sugar
½ cup flour
2 tablespoons brandy (optional)
1 tablespoon lemon juice
2 teaspoons vanilla
1½ teaspoons ground cinnamon

Streusel Topping:
½ cup chopped walnuts
½ cup almond brickle chips
⅓ cup packed brown sugar
¼ cup butter, softened
2 tablespoons flour
1½ teaspoons ground cinnamon

Preheat oven to 350° F. **To prepare Pastry Crust:** Combine flour and salt in bowl or in work bowl of food processor fitted with metal blade. Cut butter and shortening into flour with pastry blender or on/off pulses of food processor until mixture resembles coarse crumbs. Add optional cheese. Add water, a few tablespoons at a time, until dough just holds together. Form into a flat disk, wrap in wax paper and refrigerate at least 30 minutes. Roll on lightly floured surface to fit pan. Re-roll scraps and cut apple garnish; set aside. Prick pie crust with a fork. Bake 10 minutes. To prepare Filling: In large skillet, melt butter. Add apples, raisins, both sugars, flour, brandy, lemon juice, vanilla and cinnamon. Cook until apples are soft but not mushy. Allow to cool while preparing streusel topping. **To prepare Topping:** Mix all ingredients until mixture resembles coarse crumbs. Spoon filling into partially baked crust. Sprinkle with streusel topping. Place apple cut-out on top of pie. Bake pie 35-40 minutes or until bubbly and streusel top is crisp. Cool before serving.

Makes 8 servings.

Note: This pie is piled high with chunky filling—it may not cut into perfect slices.

This recipe is an adaptation of a favorite onion dip, so popular with party-goers for years. But we've given our appetizer a pretty shape in the Wilton Ring Mold Pan and added fresh vegetables for crunch. The result is a more festive, more delicious party spread. This recipe makes an ample quantity so it's perfect for any large party or picnic. Make it a day in advance then transport it conveniently in the Wilton Cake Saver Set, placed securely in a cooler. Unmold just before serving and provide assorted crackers or cut up vegetables for spreading.

Confetti Onion Ring

Wilton 10½ in. Ring Mold Pan
6 packages (8 oz. each) cream cheese, softened
1 container (16 oz.) sour cream
3 tablespoons lemon juice
2 envelopes dried onion soup mix
½ lb. carrots, peeled and finely shredded, divided
½ lb. radishes, finely shredded and squeezed dry, divided
½ cup chopped fresh parsley

Spray pan with non-stick vegetable pan spray. Line with plastic wrap. In large bowl, beat cream cheese with electric mixer on low speed until creamy. Add sour cream, lemon juice, dry soup mix, half of the carrots and half of the radishes; mix well. Sprinkle parsley in bottom of ring mold. Top parsley with 2½ cups of the cheese mixture and spread evenly. Sprinkle remaining carrots over cheese mixture; top with 2½ cups cheese mixture and spread evenly. Sprinkle remaining radishes over cheese mixture; top with remaining cheese mixture and spread evenly. Refrigerate until firm, at least 8 hours or overnight. Unmold onto serving tray. Serve with vegetables or assorted crackers.

Makes 25 appetizer-size servings.

Here's the perfect make-and-take tuna salad for your next office potluck lunch, salad supper, or family brunch. It features the same flavorful ingredients as the classic French Nicoise Salad—tuna, green beans, red potatoes, ripe olives, hard-cooked eggs, and vinaigrette dressing. But its stylish presentation comes from the Wilton Viennese Swirl Pan. Make this salad the night before and carry it to your event in the pan in a cooler (see pg. 94-95). Invert it onto a platter just before serving—the pretty garnish is instantly ready.

French Tuna Salad

Wilton Viennese Swirl Pan

Vinaigrette:
4 hard-boiled eggs, peeled
⅓ cup white balsamic or wine vinegar
1 tablespoon Dijon mustard
1 teaspoon lemon juice
½ teaspoon salt
⅛ teaspoon black pepper
⅔ cup olive oil

Salad:
2 cans (12½ oz. each) tuna packed in water, drained, flaked
3-4 small red potatoes (approximately 1 lb.), boiled, peeled and finely chopped
1 cup chopped green beans plus 12 whole beans, lightly steamed
2 green onions, sliced
⅓ cup sliced pitted black olives
1- 1½ teaspoons salt
¼-½ teaspoon black pepper

Spray pan with non stick vegetable pan spray. Line with plastic wrap. **To make Vinaigrette:** Mash egg yolks from 3 eggs. Chop whites; set aside. Reserve fourth egg for garnish. In small bowl, combine mashed egg yolks, vinegar, Dijon mustard, lemon juice, salt and pepper. Slowly whisk in olive oil. Set aside. **To prepare Salad:** Line each swirl of prepared pan with 1 whole green bean. Slice reserved egg and place in a circle around center of pan. In large bowl, combine reserved chopped egg whites, tuna, chopped green beans, potatoes, onions, olives, salt and pepper. Stir in Vinaigrette; mix well. Spoon into prepared pan; press firmly to pack. Cover with plastic wrap. Chill several hours or overnight. Invert onto serving plate.

Makes 10-12 servings.

Whether you're an occasional baker or a cook known for spectacular desserts, you'll want to bring this fresh fruit cobbler to your next potluck or church social. Its tart, luscious medley of fresh apples, pears, blueberries and raspberries is baked beneath a flaky cinnamon pastry. Prepare this delicious dessert in our Excelle® Sheet Pan with convenient see-through cover. Excelle Bakeware has a double non-stick coating that keeps baked fruit from sticking and makes cleanup a breeze.

Mixed Fruit Cobbler

Excelle 9x13-in. Sheet Pan With Cover Set

Cinnamon Pastry:

1½ cups flour
1 teaspoon sugar
1 teaspoon ground cinnamon
½ teaspoon salt
½ cup shortening
5-6 tablespoons ice water

Fruit Filling:

4 Granny Smith apples
  (approximately 1¼ lb.),
  peeled, cored and sliced
4 Bartlett pears
  (approximately 1¼ lb.)
  peeled, cored and sliced
1 pint fresh blueberries
1 pint fresh raspberries
2 cups sugar
⅔ cup flour
2 tablespoons lemon juice
2 tablespoons butter
1 cup chopped walnuts
2 tablespoons confectioners sugar

Preheat oven to 350° F. **To prepare Pastry:** Combine flour, sugar, cinnamon and salt in medium mixing bowl. Cut in shortening with pastry blender until mixture is crumbly. Add ice water, 1 tablespoon at a time, and mix with a fork until mixture holds together in a ball. Roll pastry on lightly floured surface to 13 x 12-inch rectangle, about ⅛-inch thick. Cut dough into eleven 13-inch strips. Cover with clean cloth while making filling.

To prepare Fruit Filling: Combine apples, pears, blueberries and raspberries in a large bowl. Combine sugar and flour and stir into fruit. Spread fruit mixture evenly into pan. Sprinkle with lemon juice and dot with butter. Criss-cross eight pastry strips over fruit mixture (cut two to fit short corners). Using remaining three strips, make an edge around inside rim of pan, folding over ends of strips. Combine walnuts and confectioners sugar. Sprinkle over pastry. Bake 60-70 minutes or until pastry is crusty and filling is bubbly and thickened. Serve with whipped cream, if desired.

Makes 12 servings.

If you'd like to send homemade greetings to faraway friends and relatives, but think sending a cake impossible, try these two recipes. Chocolate Fudge Cake, designed to be baked and sent in a sturdy covered cake pan, is really a double gift—the cake and the pan set. Just remember to tape the lid down for extra protection when shipping. Wilton has a wide assortment of novelty candles like those shown here, so for birthday occasions be sure to include a set. Our truly feminine heart cake is baked in the Embossed Heart Pan. It's a vision of sweet simplicity with its rolled fondant covering and icing flowers, both ready-to-use products from Wilton. What an elegant surprise for a special someone! For tips on mailing gifts of food see page 94.

Chocolate Fudge Cake To Go

Wilton 9x13-in. Covered Cake Pan

Cake:
2 cups unsifted
    all-purpose flour
2 cups sugar
1 teaspoon baking powder
1 teaspoon baking soda
½ teaspoon salt
1 teaspoon vanilla
¾ cup butter or margarine,
    room temperature
1½ cups milk
3 eggs
3 ounces unsweetened
    chocolate, melted

Icing:
1 package (14 oz.)
    Wilton Candy Melts®*,
    Dark or Light Cocoa
1 cup miniature marshmallows
½ cup whipping cream
2 tablespoons butter
½ cup chopped walnuts

Preheat oven to 350° F. Do not grease pan. **To prepare Cake:** Place all ingredients in large mixing bowl; mix at low speed of electric mixer to blend. Increase speed to medium; beat 3 minutes. Pour batter into pan. Bake 45-50 minutes or until top springs back when touched lightly in center. While cake is baking **prepare Icing:** Combine candy, marshmallows and cream in microwave-safe bowl. Microwave on MEDIUM in 1 minute cycle, stirring between, until smooth. Stir in butter and nuts. Set aside. Completely cool cake on wire rack (leave cake in pan). Frost cake with Icing. (If Icing is too thick to spread when ready to ice, warm in microwave on MEDIUM 30-45 seconds.)

Makes 12 servings.

Traveling Heart Cake

Wilton Embossed Heart Pan
Wilton 16 in. Cake Board
Wilton Ready-To-Use Rolled Fondant
Wilton Ready-To-Use Icing Roses and Rose Buds

1½ cups butter, room temperature
2½ cups sugar
5 eggs
1 teaspoon vanilla
¼ teaspoon almond extract
3 cups all-purpose flour
¾ teaspoon baking powder
¼ teaspoon salt
1 cup milk
Buttercream Icing (See pg. 66)
¼ cup apricot preserves (to seal
    cake for fondant)

Preheat oven to 350° F. Grease and flour pan. In large bowl, cream butter and sugar until light and fluffy. Add eggs, one at a time, mixing well after each addition. Stir in vanilla and almond extract. Mix flour with baking powder and salt. Add flour mixture alternately with milk, starting with flour mixture. Pour into prepared pan. Bake 45-60 minutes or until toothpick inserted in center comes out clean. Cut cake board in heart shape ¼ inch smaller than cake. Spread approximately 3 tablespoons buttercream icing on board. Trim crown of cake, if necessary, so that cake is level. Place cake on cake board. Heat preserves over low heat until melted; brush over cake. Roll fondant into 15-inch circle; drape over cake and smooth. Trim excess. (Refer to package directions for additional tips on using rolled fondant.) Place cake on covered board. Decorate with roses and rose buds.

Makes 12 servings.

Variation: Substitute 1 package yellow cake mix (2-layer size) and follow directions on package for pound cake variation.

Congratulations Jim & Mary

Here's an easy recipe for a special appetizer that is healthy but delicious. This White Bean Appetizer Heart features a well-seasoned spinach and bean filling in a light crust and is a healthy gift choice to anyone watching their fat and cholesterol intakes. Add a gift of white wine and you have a nice way to say "Congratulations" on an Engagement, New Job or Promotion. You'll find this recipe is special enough to bring to any party gathering. With a Wilton Heart Pan, you'll discover many other heart healthy ways to cook creatively. Use it for gelatin fruit salads, romantic meringue desserts, reduced fat cakes, and layered frozen yogurt creations.

White Bean Appetizer Heart

Wilton 9 in. Heart Pan
1 can (15.5 ounces) Great
    Northern White Beans
1 lb. fresh spinach, lightly
    steamed, well drained and
    chopped OR 1 package
    (10 oz.) frozen chopped spinach,
    thawed, well drained
1 tablespoon white wine vinegar
1 tablespoon olive oil
1 tablespoon finely chopped onion
1 tablespoon chopped fresh basil
2 tablespoons drained and
    chopped roasted sweet red
    pepper PLUS 1 whole piece,
    drained and sliced (for garnish)
½-¾ teaspoon salt
¼ teaspoon black pepper
1 can (10 oz.) refrigerated pizza
    crust dough
Olive oil
Herb or parsley sprigs
    (optional)

Drain beans and mash. Stir in spinach, wine vinegar, 1 tablespoon olive oil, onion, basil, chopped roasted red pepper, salt and black pepper. Refrigerate 1 hour or overnight. Preheat oven to 425° F. Roll dough out to 15x10-inch rectangle. Press dough into bottom and up 1 inch on sides of pan, trimming edges. Prick bottom with fork and refrigerate 10 minutes. Lightly brush crust with olive oil. Bake 10-12 minutes or until golden brown and crisp. Remove from pan; cool. When ready to serve, spread bean mixture into cooled crust. Garnish top with red pepper strips and herbs, if desired.

Makes 10 appetizer servings.

Folks cutting back on sugar or fat can still enjoy a sweet snack. These chewy bars, prepared with sugar substitutes and naturally sweet fruit spread, make it possible to have a low-sugar treat that tastes indulgent. Packaged in a colorful gift container, they'll be an appreciated gift for many occasions. Angel food cakes are the perfect no-fat dessert, especially when given with the season's first berries. Mini cakes are ideal—wrapped air tight and frozen, they can be taken from the freezer when needed.

No Sugar Fruit Bars

Performance Pans®
9x13-in. Sheet Pan

Crust:
1½ cups all-purpose flour
½ cup quick cooking oats
2 packages sugar substitute
   (suitable for baking)
½ cup margarine
¼ cup butter
½ teaspoon baking soda
1 egg

Topping:
½ cup flaked unsweetened
   coconut
½ cup finely chopped walnuts
¼ cup all-purpose flour
½ teaspoon brown sugar
   substitute (suitable for baking)
2 tablespoons margarine, softened
½ teaspoon ground cinnamon
1 jar (10 oz.) naturally sweetened
   fruit spread

Heat oven to 350° F. Spray pan with non-stick vegetable pan spray. **To prepare Crust:** In large bowl, combine all crust ingredients. Beat at low speed of electric mixer, scraping bowl often, until mixture is crumbly, about 1 to 2 minutes. Press onto bottom of prepared pan. Bake 18-22 minutes or until edges are lightly browned. **To prepare Topping:** In same bowl, combine coconut, walnuts, flour, brown sugar substitute, margarine and cinnamon. Beat at low speed, scraping bowl often, until well mixed; set aside. Spread fruit spread over hot crust to within ¼-inch of edges. (To make fruit spread more spreadable, heat in microwave on High for 30 seconds.) Sprinkle Topping mixture over fruit spread. Continue baking 15-20 minutes or until edges are lightly browned. Cool. Cut into bars.

Makes 2-3 dozen bars.

Mini Angel Food Cake & Fresh Strawberries

Wilton Mini Angel Food Pan

6 egg whites
¾ teaspoon cream of tartar
⅛ teaspoon salt
¾ cup granulated sugar
¾ teaspoon vanilla extract
¼ teaspoon almond extract
½ cup cake flour

Heat oven to 350° F. In a large mixing bowl, beat egg whites, cream of tartar and salt at high speed until foamy. Add sugar a little at a time; continue beating until whites are glossy and are stiff. Beat in vanilla and almond extract. Sprinkle flour over egg whites and gently fold until flour disappears. Pour batter into ungreased pan, filling cavities about ¼" from the top. Gently cut through batter with a metal spatula. Bake 25-30 minutes or until golden brown and top springs back when touched with finger. Invert cake on cooling rack. Cool completely, about 1½ hours. In one continuous motion, loosen cake from pan with narrow spatula or knife and gently shake onto serving plate.

Variation: May use same recipe to fill 7" angel food cake pan. Bake in 350° F oven 25-30 minutes.

Gifts from your kitchen can be generous and cheerful expressions of your concern for families in need, elderly neighbors, or friends returning home from the hospital. On the next six pages you'll find the recipes for two complete freeze ahead meals. The components ... casseroles, breads, and desserts...are simple. But, the intriguing flavors will say you've put some special thought into this gift. The recipes contain directions for wrapping and freezing these foods, as well as the reheating instructions. For a special touch, add pans with your gift– the 7 x 11 Sheet Pan for casseroles, the Petite Loaf Pan for breads and the Excelle 9 in. Round Pan for dessert. Your recipients will appreciate knowing there's a home cooked meal in their freezer just ready to be reheated and enjoyed in its own pan. Start with these two casseroles—tasty and convenient one-dish meals.

Basil Cinnamon Chicken Casserole

Performance Pans® 7x11-in. Sheet Pan

¼ cup olive oil
4 boneless, skinless chicken breast halves (approximately 1½ lb.)
2 teaspoons dried basil leaves
1 teaspoon ground cinnamon
1 large Spanish onion, sliced
1 cup peeled baby carrots (approximately ½ lb.)
1 can (10 ½ oz.) double strength chicken broth, undiluted
½ lb. rotini noodles, cooked
1 can (10 ½ oz.) condensed cream of chicken soup, undiluted
1 teaspoon salt
¼ teaspoon ground black pepper

Line pan with foil. Heat oil in large skillet over medium heat. Add chicken and cook until lightly browned. Stir in basil and cinnamon, turning chicken to coat. Remove chicken; keep warm. Add onions to pan and cook about 5 minutes or until crisp-tender, stirring frequently. Stir in carrots and chicken broth. Cover and cook 5-10 minutes or until carrots are tender. Add rotini, soup, salt and pepper to pan; mix lightly. Place mixture in prepared pan, top with chicken. Cover pan with foil; freeze. When frozen, remove casserole from pan, overwrap in freezer wrap or foil and store for up to two months.

To bake frozen casserole, preheat oven to 350° F. Remove overwrap and foil and place frozen casserole in 7x11-inch pan. Cover loosely with foil to keep moist. Bake frozen casserole 1½ hours to 2 hours or until thoroughly heated. **To bake without freezing**, preheat oven to 350° F. Cover loosely with foil. Bake 30 to 35 minutes or until thoroughly heated.

Makes 4 servings.

Orange Spiced Pork Bake

Performance Pans® 7x11-in. Sheet Pan

1 whole pork tenderloin (approximately 1¼ lb.)
2 tablespoons vegetable oil
1 teaspoon paprika
Salt and pepper to taste
1 large Spanish onion, sliced
1 cup sliced celery
½ cup orange juice (undiluted concentrated juice)
2 tablespoons honey
2 cups cooked long grain and wild rice with seasoning packet (6.25 oz. pkg.)
1 can (10 ¾ oz.) condensed cream of celery soup, undiluted
1 cup petite peas
1 jar (4½ oz.) sliced mushrooms, drained
¼ cup chopped red pepper

Line pan with foil. Slice pork into 1-inch slices; press with palm of hand to flatten. Heat oil in large skillet. Sprinkle pork with paprika, salt and pepper. Cook over medium-high heat until browned on both sides. Remove pork from skillet. Add onion, celery, orange juice, honey to skillet; cook until onions are tender (about 5 minutes). Stir in rice mixture, soup, peas, mushrooms, red pepper, salt and pepper. Place in prepared pan, top with browned pork. Cover with foil; freeze. When frozen, remove casserole from pan, overwrap in freezer wrap or foil and store for up to two months. Follow baking directions in recipe above.

Makes 4 servings.

Wholesome breads, especially savory petite loaves, are pleasant meal accompaniments. Be sure to add our cheesy biscuit bread and peppery corn bread to your dinner gift basket. You can mix and match these individual-sized loaves with either of the casseroles on the previous page. Both recipes are quick and easy to prepare and bake up golden brown in Wilton's Petite Loaf Pan. Wrapped in foil and frozen, they'll reheat beautifully for fresh-from-the-oven flavor.

Buttermilk Biscuit Bread With Cheese

Wilton 9 Cavity Petite Loaf Pan
2 cups flour
1 tablespoon chopped chives
2 teaspoons baking powder
¼ teaspoon baking soda
¼ teaspoon salt
¼ cup butter or margarine
¾ cup finely shredded sharp cheddar cheese, divided
1¼ cups buttermilk

Preheat oven to 350° F. Generously grease pan. In medium bowl, combine flour, chives, baking powder, baking soda and salt. Cut in butter with a pastry blender until mixture is crumbly. Stir in ½ cup cheese. Add buttermilk, mixing just until dry ingredients are moistened. Spoon dough into prepared pan. Sprinkle with the remaining ¼ cup cheese. Bake 30 to 35 minutes or until lightly browned. Run sharp knife around each loaf to loosen. Cool on wire racks. Wrap cooled loaves in foil; freeze. When ready to serve, heat foil-wrapped loaves in 350° F oven 25-30 minutes or until warmed.

Makes 9 petite loaves.

Cracked Pepper Corn Bread

Wilton 9 Cavity Petite Loaf Pan
1 cup flour
1 cup yellow cornmeal
2 tablespoons sugar
2 teaspoons baking powder
1 teaspoon salt
¾ teaspoon coarsely cracked mixed peppercorns
1 can (8.5 oz.) creamed corn
1 cup milk
2 tablespoons butter, melted
1 egg, beaten

Preheat oven to 375° F. Spray pan with non stick vegetable pan spray. In medium bowl, combine flour, cornmeal, sugar, baking powder, salt and peppercorns. In small bowl, combine corn, milk, melted butter and egg. Add to flour mixture and mix just until dry ingredients are moistened. Spoon dough into prepared pan. Bake 25 to 30 minutes or until centers spring back when lightly touched and edges are lightly browned. Cool on wire racks. Wrap cooled loaves in foil; freeze. When ready to serve, heat foil-wrapped loaves in 350° F oven 25-30 minutes or until warmed.

Makes 9 petite loaves.

DESSERTS:

Peach Gingerbread
Papaya-Pineapple
Upside Down Cake

Round out your dinner gift basket with two cozy homemade desserts. Peach Gingerbread With Lemon Rosemary Sauce and Pineapple Papaya Upside Down Cake are delicious updated versions of old-fashioned favorites. Both are baked in the Excelle® 9 inch Round Cake Pan with double non-stick coating (making clean up a breeze). The cakes are baked and then frozen; the sauce is refrigerated. Either dessert complements the other casseroles and mini loaves. Finally, make your dinner gift basket extra special with a bottle of wine, a bouquet of fresh flowers, elegant disposable plates and napkins, pretty candles, flavored coffees, or after dinner candies. And don't forget to include the baking pan and recipes for all the delicious gifts from your kitchen.

Peach Gingerbread

Excelle 9 in. Round Cake Pan

1¾ cups flour
1 teaspoon baking powder
¼ teaspoon baking soda
1½ teaspoons ground ginger
1 teaspoon ground cinnamon
½ teaspoon salt
½ cup butter or margarine
½ cup sugar
1 egg
½ cup light molasses
½ cup sour milk or buttermilk
1 can (16 oz.) sliced peaches in light
   syrup, drained, cut into chunks

Preheat oven to 350° F. Spray pan with non stick vegetable pan spray. Combine flour, baking powder, baking soda, ginger, cinnamon and salt. Set aside. In medium bowl, beat butter and sugar until creamy. Beat in egg and molasses. Add dry ingredients alternately with buttermilk, mixing until well blended. Stir in peaches. Pour mixture into prepared pan. Bake 40-45 minutes or until cake springs back when lightly touched in center and edges begin to pull away from sides of pan. Cool 5 minutes in pan; invert and cool, right-side up, on wire rack. Serve cake with Lemon Rosemary Sauce. To freeze, wrap tightly in foil and label. Reheat pan at 350°F for 20-25 minutes.

Makes 8 servings.

Lemon Rosemary Sauce

⅓ cup butter, melted
½ cup sugar
¼ cup lemon juice
1 egg, beaten
1 tablespoon grated lemon peel
1 teaspoon finely chopped fresh
   rosemary leaves OR 1 teaspoon
   dried rosemary

Combine all ingredients in small saucepan. Cook over medium heat, stirring constantly, until mixture boils and thickens. Cool. Store in refrigerator until ready to serve.

Makes 1 cup.

Papaya Pineapple Upside Down Cake

Excelle 9 in. Round Cake Pan

Topping:
¼ cup butter or margarine, melted
½ cup packed brown sugar
1 can (8 oz.) pineapple rings,
   drained (reserve juice)
¼ papaya, peeled and sliced
¼ cup blanched sliced almonds

Cake:
1½ cups flour
1 teaspoon baking powder
¼ teaspoon salt
½ cup butter or margarine
¼ cup granulated sugar
2 eggs, beaten
1 teaspoon vanilla extract
Reserved pineapple juice
Water

Preheat oven to 350° F. Spray pan with non stick vegetable pan spray. **To prepare Topping:** Combine melted butter and brown sugar. Spread evenly in prepared pan. Arrange pineapple and papaya slices over butter and sugar mixture. Decorate with almonds. **To prepare Cake:** Combine flour, baking powder and salt. Set aside. In large bowl, beat butter and sugar until creamy. Beat in eggs, one at a time, until well blended. Stir in vanilla. Pour reserved pineapple juice into glass measuring cup. Add enough water to make ½ cup. Add flour mixture to butter mixture alternately with juice, mixing until well blended. Pour batter over pineapple and papaya slices in pan. Bake 30-35 minutes or until golden brown and wooden pick inserted near center comes out clean. Cool 10 minutes in pan; invert onto serving platter. To freeze, invert on foil, cool, wrap and freeze. Reheat in pan in 350°F oven for 20-25 minutes.

Makes 9 servings.

the kitchen of: Sandy

Peach Muff

1/4 cup whole wheat flour
1/4 cup all-purpose flour
1 tsp. baking powder
a pinch of salt
1/4 cup low-fat

serves: 12

Singles, young couples, and empty-nesters all share the challenges of small scale cooking. Featured here are two recipes, turkey meat loaf and peach muffins, especially suitable for small quantity cooking. These foods, with their recipes and the accompanying bakeware, make a wonderful "housewarming" gift for couples setting up their first apartment or downsizing to a retirement condo. The lean turkey meat loaf is prepared in the Excelle® Meat Loaf Set—a pan and drip rack—perfect for making meat loaves with less fat. Our healthy peach muffins are baked in the Excelle Mini Muffin Pan. These pans each fit in a toaster oven—a great energy-saver when cooking for one or two.

Turkey Meat Loaf

Excelle Meat Loaf Pan with Drip Rack Set

1½ lbs. fresh ground turkey
½ -¾ cup fresh bread crumbs
1 egg white
¼ cup chopped onion
¼ cup chopped red pepper
2 tablespoons chopped parsley
1 tablespoon white wine
    Worcestershire sauce
½ teaspoon seasoned salt
½ teaspoon salt
¼ teaspoon garlic powder
¼ teaspoon onion powder
⅛ teaspoon black pepper
2 tablespoons tomato paste
2 tablespoons water

Preheat toaster oven to 350° F. Lightly spray drip pan with non stick vegetable pan spray. Combine all ingredients except tomato paste and water; mix lightly. Shape into loaf in prepared pan. Bake 15 minutes. Spread combined tomato paste and water over meat loaf; continue baking 15-20 minutes more or until juices run clear. Garnish with green, red and yellow pepper strips, if desired.

Makes 4 servings.

Variation: Substitute ground beef for ground turkey. May need to increase baking time.

Note: Slice leftover meat loaf for sandwiches.

Low Fat Peach Muffins

Excelle Mini Muffin Pan

¼ cup all-purpose flour
¼ cup whole wheat flour
1 teaspoon baking powder
Pinch of salt
¼ cup low fat peach yogurt
2 tablespoons chopped dried
    peaches
2 tablespoons honey
1 teaspoon vegetable oil
1 egg white
½ teaspoon vanilla
1 tablespoon honey crunch
    wheat germ

Preheat toaster oven to 350° F. Spray pan with non stick vegetable pan spray. In medium bowl, combine all-purpose flour, whole wheat flour, baking powder and salt; mix well. In small bowl, combine yogurt, peaches, honey, oil, egg white and vanilla; mix well. Add to dry ingredients; stir just until dry ingredients are moistened. Fill cups of muffin pan ½ full. Sprinkle with wheat germ. Bake 8-10 minutes.

Makes 12 mini muffins.

Share your passion for chocolate with elegant cakes and melt-in-your-mouth candy. Deliciously dense chocolate cake in miniature size, makes a beautiful gift for a hostess, teacher, or grandmother. The Wilton Mini Shell Pan gives the cakes their delicate shape.

Wrapped individually in fancy gold boxes, these packages are almost too pretty to open. The layered chocolate mint candy, made with Wilton Candy Melts, is really a no-fuss confection. It's so easy to make, you won't want to wait for special occasions to give it away.

Mini Chocolate Shell Cakes

Wilton Mini Shell Pan
Wilton Tip 102
Wilton Disposable
*   Decorating Bags*
Unsweetened cocoa
1¼ cups semi-sweet
*   chocolate chips*
¼ cup butter
1 tablespoon flour
1 tablespoon sugar
½ teaspoon vanilla
2 eggs, slightly beaten
2 tablespoons finely chopped
*   walnuts (optional)*
Confectioners sugar
Buttercream icing, tinted with
*   Wilton Pink Icing Color*
*   (see page 66)*

Preheat oven to 350° F. Spray pan with non stick vegetable pan spray; generously dust pan with cocoa powder. In 2-quart saucepan, melt chocolate chips with butter over low heat, stirring constantly, until chocolate is melted (about 4-5 minutes). Stir in flour, sugar and vanilla. Stir in eggs, one at a time, and mix until well blended. Stir in walnuts. Pour batter into prepared pan. Bake 10-12 minutes or until toothpick inserted in center comes out clean. Cool 10-15 minutes in pan on wire rack before removing. Cool. Cakes are delicious stored in the refrigerator and served chilled. To garnish, sprinkle with confectioners sugar and make buttercream icing ribbon, using tip 102 and decorating bags, if desired. To make decorative garnish with confectioners sugar as shown in photo, shape piece of foil around shell on back of pan. Remove foil. Cut narrow lengthwise slits in foil with small scissors. Mold foil over shell cake. Use a small sieve to sprinkle confectioners sugar over cake. Carefully remove foil. Re-shape foil over back of pan after each use. Repeat with remaining cakes.

Makes 6 shell cakes.

Triple Layer Mint Chocolate Candy

Excelle 8 in. Square Cake Pan
1 package (14 oz.) Wilton Candy
*   Melts®*, Dark Cocoa Mint*
7 ounces (½ pkg.) Wilton Candy
*   Melts®*, Green*

*Brand confectionery coating

Melt candy in separate containers according to package directions. Pour one half melted cocoa mint flavored candy in pan; refrigerate 5 minutes. Top with melted green candy; refrigerate 5 minutes. Add remaining melted cocoa mint flavored candy and swirl top. Refrigerate until set, about 5-10 minutes. Unmold from pan and place, swirled-side up, on cutting board. Let candy come to room temperature; cut into squares or diamonds.

Makes about 36 pieces.

Casual entertaining is in style these days with simple menus and unpretentious foods. But even hostesses of informal get togethers appreciate guests who bring a dish to share. Cheese spreads are always popular, especially ones with south-of-the-border flair. This spread takes only minutes to make and needs just an hour to chill for flavors to blend. Use Wilton Mini Pans to mold this spicy cheddar spread into special shapes. Take along a selection of crackers and vegetables for spreading.

Spicy Cheddar Spread

*Wilton Shortcakes 'N
    Treats Pan or*
Wilton Mini Ball Pan
*2 cups (8 oz.) shredded medium
    sharp cheddar cheese*
*1 package (8 oz.) cream
    cheese, softened*
*3 tablespoons packaged taco
    seasoning mix (or to taste)*
*3 tablespoons canned chopped
    green chilies*
*¾ cup finely chopped
    walnuts (optional)*

Line cavities of pans with plastic wrap. In food processor fitted with steel blade or mixing bowl, combine all ingredients except chilies and walnuts. Blend thoroughly. Stir in chilies. Press into cavities of pans. (To make mini balls, roll mixture into walnuts before pressing into cavities of pan.) Cover with plastic wrap. Chill 1 hour or overnight. Unmold onto serving tray. To decorate mini balls, fill disposable decorating bag with softened cream cheese and pipe tip 16 stars.

Makes approximately 2½ cups mixture, enough for 4-5 cheese balls.

Note: For fancy-cut vegetables, use Wilton Bite-Size Cookie Cutters. Good vegetables to use include bell peppers, cucumbers, yellow squash, and zucchini.

To tease the appetite, olive bread and savory feta cheese paté make a lively pair. For intimate dinner parties, small receptions or celebrations, housewarmings or gatherings before a night on the town, this appetizer will be a gift welcomed by your hostess. Both the bread and paté, inspired with flavors from Greece, are prepared in the Wilton Mini Loaf Pan. Because the recipes make six each of the bread and paté, they make ideal presents to give during the busy holiday entertaining season. You can even avoid the last minute rush by preparing the bread in advance and freezing.

Feta Cheese & Vegetable Paté

Wilton 6 Cavity Mini Loaf Pan

2 envelopes unflavored gelatin
½ cup cold water
10 oz. feta cheese, crumbled
2 packages (8 oz. each) cream cheese, softened
¼ cup half-and-half
1 medium leek, cleaned and sliced (about 1½ cups)
1 tablespoon margarine
½ teaspoon dried tarragon leaves
2 teaspoons chopped fresh parsley
1 can (8 oz.) sliced beets, well drained (about ¾ cup)
¼ teaspoon dry mustard
⅛ teaspoon ground cloves

Brush cavities of pan with oil; set aside. Sprinkle gelatin over water in glass measuring cup. Let stand 2 minutes to soften. Heat in microwave on HIGH for 4 minutes. Let stand for 2 minutes or until dissolved; stir. Crumble feta cheese into food processor bowl fitted with steel blade. Process to very fine crumbs. Add dissolved gelatin, cream cheese and half-and-half; process until smooth. Spread ¼ cup cheese mixture evenly into each cavity. Divide remaining mixture in half; set aside. Sauté or microwave leeks in margarine until tender. Stir in tarragon and parsley. Pureé in food processor; add to half of cheese mixture. Spread about ¼ cup leek mixture evenly into each cavity. Pureé beets with mustard and cloves in food processor; add to remaining cheese mixture. Spread about ¼ cup beet mixture into each cavity. Chill several hours or overnight. Unmold onto plate; garnish with fresh herbs. Serve with Greek Olive Bread.

Makes 6 mini loaf patés.

Greek Olive Bread

Wilton 6 Cavity Mini Loaf Pan

1 package (16 oz.) hot roll mix
4 ounces (¼ cup) Greek olives, pitted, coarsely chopped
1 teaspoon dried oregano leaves
¼ teaspoon garlic powder
⅛ teaspoon ground nutmeg
1 cup hot water (120-130°F)
2 tablespoons butter or margarine, softened
1 egg
Olive oil (optional)

Spray pan with non-stick vegetable pan spray. In large bowl, combine hot roll mix, yeast packet, olives, oregano, garlic powder and nutmeg; mix well. Stir in hot water, butter and egg until dough sticks together to form a ball. Turn dough onto lightly floured surface. With floured hands, shape dough into a large ball. Knead 5 minutes or until smooth. Cover with a large bowl and let rest 5 minutes. Divide dough into six equal portions. Shape gently into small loaves and place in prepared pan. Cover with a clean cloth and let rise in warm place until doubled in bulk. Preheat oven to 375°F. Make three crosswise slashes on top of each loaf. Bake 15 to 20 minutes or until golden brown. Remove from pan and cool on wire rack. Brush tops of loaves lightly with olive oil, if desired.

Makes 6 mini loaves.

Sometimes a gift from the heart, for no reason at all, is the most precious. These spicy gingerbread cookies with delicate trims are appropriate for just those times, when you simply want to say, "I'm Thinking Of You." To make these old-fashioned gingerbread cookies, simply press the dough into Wilton's elegant Mini Embossed Heart Pan. Use Royal Icing to create lacy outlines, accent the centers with piped rosebuds or charming handpainted designs. Make them as simple or elaborate as you like, then package them in fine tins or boxes.

Gingerbread Cookies

Wilton Mini Embossed
    Heart Pan
Wilton Golden Yellow, Moss
    Green Icing Colors
Wilton Disposable
    Decorating Bags
Wilton Tips 1, 2, 101
Wilton Clear Vanilla Extract
Wilton Decorator Brush Set
4 to 4½ cups all-purpose
    flour, divided
⅔ cup molasses
½ cup packed brown sugar
½ cup butter, room temperature
2 eggs
½ teaspoon baking soda
½ teaspoon salt
½ teaspoon ground allspice
½ teaspoon ground cinnamon
½ teaspoon ground cloves
½ teaspoon ground ginger
Royal Icing (see below)

Preheat oven to 375° F. Spray pan with non-stick vegetable pan spray. In large bowl, mix 1½ cups flour and remaining ingredients at low speed of electric mixer until well blended, scraping bowl often. Increase speed to medium and beat two minutes or until very smooth. Reduce speed to low; add remaining flour, 1 cup at a time, until dough is very stiff. If you are using a portable mixer the last flour may need to be stirred or kneaded in by hand. Press approximately ¼ cup dough into each cavity. Dough should be ¼ inch thick. Bake 8-10 minutes or until lightly browned at edges. Cool 5 minutes on wire rack. Loosen edges with small spatula; invert. Let cool completely before decorating. **To Decorate:** Using thinned royal icing and tips 1 and 2, fill in center and make lines and dots. Let set until icing is firm before painting (overnight is best). For cookies pictured on cover: Using icing color thinned with small amount of clear vanilla*, paint flower designs. For cookies pictured here: Using tip 101, make rose buds (see Wilton Yearbook for complete instructions). Add painted stems, leaves and accents. Store in loosely covered container.

*Color should be not be thinned with water. You can substitute vodka for vanilla to thin color.

Makes 2 dozen cookies.

Royal Icing

3 level tablespoons Wilton
    Meringue Powder
4 cups sifted confectioners sugar
    (approximately 1 lb.)
6 tablespoons water*

*When using large counter top
    mixer or for stiffer icing, use 1
    tablespoon less water

Beat all ingredients at low speed for 7-10 minutes (10-12 minutes at high speed for portable mixer) until icing forms peaks.

Makes 3 cups.

If you're a bird watcher or dog lover, here are some special treats you can make for your animal friends. For his devoted loyalty and friendship, reward your dog with nothing but the best tasty homemade dog biscuits. A Wilton Cookie Cutter is used to cut the biscuit dough in the traditional shape, a dog bone, of course. During the cold winter months our hungry bird friends need our help. Families, scout troops, or school groups can make these Bird Treats with suet, purchased from the butcher, and bird seed. The mixture is molded in Wilton's Mini Tree Pan, wrapped in net, and tied to tree branches. Or make your feathered friends a bird seed pie in your old pie pan. Then treat yourself to a new pan from Wilton.

Dog Biscuits

**Wilton Dog Bone Perimeter
Cookie Cutter**
Wilton Cookie Sheet
1 package (10 oz.)
   frozen chopped spinach,
   thawed, drained
1 cup (4 oz.) finely shredded
   mild cheddar cheese, room
   temperature
1 cup margarine, softened
2 cloves garlic, crushed
2 cups whole wheat flour
½ cup nonfat dry milk
Water (optional)

In food processor fitted with steel blade, process spinach, cheese, margarine and garlic. Add dry ingredients. Process until dough forms, adding water if necessary. Chill 1 hour. Preheat oven to 300° F. Spray cookie sheet with non stick vegetable pan spray. Roll dough out on lightly floured surface. Cut with dog bone cutter. Place on prepared cookie sheet. Bake 30-45 minutes or until lightly browned. Remove to cooling rack. Cool.

Makes 2-3 dozen.

Bird Treats

**Wilton Mini Tree Pan
or Pie Pan**
2 cups ground suet
   (approximately 1 lb.)
1 cup bird seed, sunflower
   seeds or cracked corn

Melt suet in a double boiler; set aside to cool and thicken slightly.
To make Trees: With hands, form cooled melted suet into tree shapes the approximate size of cavities in tree pan.
Press suet shapes into bird seed, then into mini tree pan. Refrigerate until hardened. Unmold. Place in mesh bags or wrap in nylon net and hang on tree branches for the birds.

Makes 4-5 trees.

Bird Pie

Double above recipe. When hardened slightly, reheat. Add 1 cup of seed and pour into pan. Sprinkle remaining seed on top. Refrigerate until firm. Be sure to set pie off the ground where birds are safe eating.

✦ PART II ✦

GIFTS
for
SPECIAL OCCASIONS

*Life is full of occasions that call
for celebration. With our help,
you can acknowledge these times
with gifts from the kitchen.*

*For Mother's Day and Father's
Day, a graduation or visit
from the stork, we have tasty
gift suggestions. From picnics
to parties, Wilton bakeware
and decorating products
will help you celebrate.*

When wedding bells are fast approaching, honor the bride-to-be with a party just for her. Whether you hostess a brunch, lunch, or tea, shower her with a gift basket of bakeware from Wilton. Include a Petite Muffin Pan and Mini Loaf Pan, just right for cooking for two. Our perforated Bread Stick Pan is great for refrigerated dough, while everyone needs a Loaf Pan for baking quick breads. New brides who like to entertain will enjoy a Springform Pan, ideal for cheesecake, quiche and more. And our Mini Umbrella Pan will remind her always of this special time in her life. End your party on an elegant note with these sweetly-decorated chocolate umbrellas. Packaged in pretty individual gift boxes, they can be presented to guests when they leave as a pleasant reminder of this happy occasion.

Bread Sticks

Wilton Bread Stick Pan
Wilton Pastry Brush
1 can (11 oz.) refrigerated
   bread sticks
2 tablespoons olive oil
3 tablespoons assorted seeds
   (mustard, sesame, poppy or dill)

Preheat oven to 350°F. Spray pan with non-stick vegetable pan spray. Unroll dough. With pastry brush, coat top of dough with oil. Sprinkle with seeds, pressing lightly. Separate strips of dough and twist. Place on alternate grooves in pan. Bake 15-20 minutes or until browned. Let cool 5 minutes; remove from pan.

Makes 8 bread sticks.

Fudge Umbrellas

Wilton Mini Umbrella Pan
Wilton Icing Colors, Pink,
   Golden Yellow and Leaf
   Green
Wilton Disposable
   Decorating Bags
Wilton Tips 0, 2, 4, 224
   and 349
1 package (14 oz.) Wilton
   Candy Melts®*, Light
   or Dark Cocoa
1 cup miniature marshmallows
½ cup whipping cream
1 cup chopped pecans
   or walnuts
Buttercream Icing (see pg. 66)

*brand confectionery coating

NOTE: For instructions on specific decorating techniques, see the current Wilton Yearbook of Cake Decorating.

Spray pan heavily with non-stick vegetable pan spray. Combine Candy Melts, cream and marshmallows in large microwave safe container. Heat on medium-high heat in 1 minute cycles, stirring between, until melted and smooth. Candy will be very thick and may look slightly rough textured. Stir in nuts. Divide mixture evenly into six cavities, about ½ inch from top. Press firmly into pans. Refrigerate until very firm, about 1½-2 hours, or freeze for 20-30 minutes. Let set at room temperature for a few minutes. Remove by running a small pointed spatula around edges of pan. Decorate with buttercream icing: Using pink buttercream and tip 4, outline umbrella. with tip 224, add pink drop flowers to tops of umbrellas. Using yellow buttercream and tip 2, add centers to drop flowers. With green buttercream and tip 349, add leaves. Store at room temperature in covered container up to one week.

Makes 6 fudge umbrellas.

New babies are a blessing, but when that bundle of joy arrives, family mealtime often turns chaotic. To help mom get a quick dinner on the table, give her this special gift basket with a family-favorite meal—Sloppy Joe Sandwiches. The sandwich buns are a convenience dough baked in Wilton's Mini Bear Pan. (These bears are fun for "big" brothers and sisters.) The prepared meat mixture should be chilled, then packaged in a microwave-safe container for easy reheating. Because both the buns and sandwich filling freeze well, they can be saved for a busy night in the future. Finally, add charm to your gift basket with a new baby decoration from the Bomboniere!® product selection, or with a homemade party favor from the Bomboniere® Party Favors! idea book.

Sloppy Joes in Mini Bear Buns

Wilton Mini Bear Pan

Buns:
1 loaf (1 lb.) frozen bread dough
    OR 1 package hot roll mix

Meat Filling:
½ cup coarsely chopped red or
    green pepper
½ cup chopped onion
2 cloves garlic, chopped
1 tablespoon vegetable oil
1 lb. ground beef
1 cup tomato sauce
¼ cup barbecue sauce (optional)
1 rounded tablespoon
    tomato paste
½ teaspoon salt
½ teaspoon black pepper

To prepare Buns: Thaw dough or prepare mix for baking according to package directions. Spray pan with non-stick vegetable pan spray. Knead dough into 6-8 balls. Place balls, smooth-side down, in pan, pressing to fit cavity. (As dough rises it will fill bear shapes.) Let dough rise, covered, in a warm place until doubled in size. Preheat oven to 350° F. Bake 15-20 minutes or until golden brown. Remove from pan; cool.

To prepare Meat Filling: Sauté red pepper, onion and garlic in oil until tender. Add ground beef and cook until no longer pink; drain fat. Stir in tomato sauce, barbecue sauce, tomato paste, salt and pepper. Simmer 20 minutes or until slightly thickened and thoroughly heated.

Makes 6 servings.

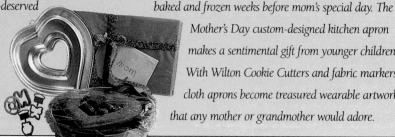

This rosy Strawberry Heart Bread, baked in our heart-shaped Ring Pan and filled with fresh strawberries, is a well-deserved treat for any mom on Mother's Day. Serve it with a strawberry butter molded in Wilton Heart Candy Molds for an added touch of elegance. Teen cooks can easily accomplish the cooking portion of this Mother's Day gift. Both recipes can be prepared a day in advance. The bread can even be baked and frozen weeks before mom's special day. The Mother's Day custom-designed kitchen apron makes a sentimental gift from younger children. With Wilton Cookie Cutters and fabric markers, cloth aprons become treasured wearable artwork that any mother or grandmother would adore.

Strawberry Heart Bread

Wilton Heart Ring Pan
3 cups flour
1½ cups sugar
1 teaspoon baking soda
½ teaspoon salt
1 tablespoon cinnamon
2 packages (10 oz. each)
    frozen strawberries, thawed,
    including juice
4 eggs
1¼ cups vegetable oil
1¼ cups chopped nuts
    (walnuts or pecans)

Preheat oven to 350° F. Spray pan with non-stick vegetable cooking spray. In large bowl, mix flour, sugar, baking soda, salt and cinnamon together. Set aside. In separate bowl, combine strawberries with juice, eggs and oil. Pour strawberry mixture into flour mixture and stir just until flour is absorbed. Stir in nuts. Pour into prepared pan. Bake 50-60 minutes or until done (toothpick inserted in bread comes out clean). Cool 10 minutes; invert onto cooling rack. Cool.

Makes 10-12 servings.

Strawberry Butter

Wilton Heart Candy Molds
2 tablespoons strawberry preserve
½ cup butter, softened

Stir preserves into butter. Press into molds; freeze until firm. Remove from molds. Store in refrigerator. Let come to room temperature before serving.

Makes ½ cup.

Mother's Day Apron

Wilton Alphabet Cookie Cutters
Wilton Apple and Butterfly
    Bite-Size Cookie Cutters
Apron
Fabric Paint and Markers

To make outline of design, brush damp sponge cloth with fabric paint. Press cutter into paint, then onto apron. Let dry a few minutes. With fabric marker, color in designs. (Use apple cookie cutter to make strawberries.) With black fabric marker, outline design. (Fabric paint can be used for complete design. However, children will find fabric markers easier to use to fill in design.) Treat apron before and after painting according to manufacturer's directions on fabric paint and markers.

No one's on a par with Dad—surprise him with this "hole-in-one" lemon cake baked in Wilton's popular 10-inch Ring Mold Pan. This delightful dessert course is easy to decorate with buttercream icing, chopped nuts, green-tinted coconut, and Wilton's Golf Cake Topper Set. Complete the golfing theme with homemade candy golf balls—"a gimme" to make with our fool-proof truffles recipe and Wilton Candy Melts.

Lemon Coconut Cake

Wilton 10-in. Ring Mold Pan
Wilton Leaf Green Icing Color
Wilton Golf Cake Topper Set

Cake:
2 cups cake flour
1 cup sugar
2 teaspoons baking powder
1 package (3 oz.) lemon gelatin
¾ cup milk
⅔ cup vegetable oil
2 tablespoons lemon extract
3 large eggs, separated
¼ cup sugar

Glaze:
1 lb. confectioners sugar
¾ cup lemon juice

Frosting:
3 cups Buttercream Icing (See pg. 66)
   OR 2 cans Wilton Ready-To-Use
   Decorator Icing
2 cups finely chopped nuts
1½ cups flaked coconut

Preheat oven to 325° F. Spray pan with non-stick vegetable cooking spray.

To prepare cake: In large mixing bowl, sift together cake flour, 1 cup sugar, baking powder and gelatin. Beat in milk, oil and lemon extract. Beat in egg yolks, one at a time. Beat egg whites until stiff, but not dry, beating in ¼ cup sugar. Fold egg whites gently, but thoroughly, into batter. Pour batter into prepared pan. Bake 30-45 minutes or until cake springs back lightly to the touch. Turn out immediately onto wire rack. While cake is baking, prepare glaze.

To prepare glaze: Combine confectioners sugar and lemon juice in saucepan; heat until very hot. Keep warm while cake is baking. Carefully and slowly spoon the warm glaze over warm cake on wire rack until all glaze is absorbed. Let cool 1 hour. While cake is cooling, tint coconut. To tint coconut, place coconut in plastic bag. Add few drops icing color and shake bag until color is evenly distributed. Frost cooled cake with buttercream icing. Press nuts around sides of cake. Sprinkle top with green-tinted coconut. Decorate with cake topper set.

Makes 10-12 servings

Golf Ball Truffles

½ cup whipping cream
1 package (14 oz.) Wilton
   Candy Melts®*, Dark Cocoa
1 tablespoon liqueur or 1 teaspoon
   flavoring of your choice (optional)
1 package (14 oz.) Wilton Candy
   Melts®*, White

*brand confectionery coating

Heat whipping cream in microwave or on top of range until almost boiling. Add Dark Cocoa candy; stir until smooth. Add liqueur or flavoring, if desired. Refrigerate until firm; form into golf ball size truffles. Refrigerate. Melt white candy according to package directions. Let cool slightly. Dip centers; place on wax paper to set. When set, dip again and roll across grid type cooling rack to make rough surface. Store in refrigerator.

Makes 14-20 truffles.

Knowing how teens love pizza, you'll get extra credit for this graduation gift from the kitchen. Our nut-filled cake with fanciful "pizza" toppings is a clever departure from the traditional grad cake. The natural packaging is a pizza box, of course.

Our Rocky Road and Tropical Pizza Pies are two other great ways to say "Good Luck" on Finals. They're made with Wilton Candy Melts®, easily molded in our Muffin Caps Pan. Topped with marshmallows, nuts, and cherries, they're as fun to make as they are to eat.

"Pizza" Cake

Wilton 10-in. Round
      Cake Pan
Wilton Golden Yellow Icing Color
Wilton Cinnamon Sprinkle
      Decorations
1 cup sugar, divided
⅔ cup butter or margarine, room
      temperature
5 large eggs, separated
½ teaspoon almond extract
2⅓ cups slivered almonds, toasted
      and coarsely chopped
½ cup fine dry bread crumbs
1 cup Buttercream Icing (see pg. 66)
⅓ cup cherry or strawberry jelly
½ cup flaked coconut
Small green gumdrops
2 teaspoons milk

Preheat oven to 350° F. Spray pan with non-stick vegetable pan spray. In large bowl, beat ¾ cup sugar with the butter until creamy. Add egg yolks, one at a time, beating well after each addition. Add almond extract. Gradually sprinkle in almonds and bread crumbs; blend well. In large bowl, beat egg whites with remaining ¼ cup sugar until whites hold stiff peaks. Stir half the whites into batter just until blended. Fold in remaining whites. Spoon batter into prepared pan. Bake 35-40 minutes or until top is golden brown and toothpick inserted in center comes out clean. Cool on rack 10 minutes before turning out. Cool completely. Reserve ¼ cup icing. Spread cake with remaining icing. Top cake with jelly to resemble pizza sauce. Sprinkle with coconut tinted with icing color for cheddar cheese. To make olives, flatten gumdrops with palm of hand or rolling pin. Cut olives with large end of tip #10, cut centers with small end of tip. Insert cinnamon candy in olive center. Arrange over cake. Thin reserved icing with milk; drizzle over cake to resemble mozzarella cheese.

Makes 12 servings.

Candy Pizzas

Crusts:
Wilton Muffin Caps Pan
1 package (14 oz.)
      Wilton Candy
  Melts®*, Light or Dark Cocoa
Tropical Pizzas:
6 candy crusts
¾ cup candied cherries
1 cup flaked coconut
4 ounces Wilton White Candy
      Melts®*, melted
Rocky Road Pizzas:
6 candy crusts
1½ cups miniature marshmallows
¼ cup chopped pecans or walnuts
4 ounces Wilton White Candy
      Melts®*, melted

To make Crusts: Melt candy according to package directions. Fill cavities of pan and refrigerate 3-4 minutes or until ¼-inch shell forms. Invert to drain excess coating. Return shells to refrigerator to set. Makes 7-8 crusts if excess coating is remelted and molded.

To make Tropical Pizzas: Top crusts with cherries and coconut. Drizzle with melted white candy. Makes 6 pizzas.

To make Rocky Road Pizzas: Top crusts with marshmallows and nuts. Drizzle with melted white candy. Makes 6 pizzas.

Remember the excitement of setting up your first apartment? Stocking the cupboards of that first kitchen was a challenge. Now you can give your favorite new cook a great culinary start with a gift of some cooking essentials–Wilton's 3-piece mixing bowl set, measuring spoon set, hardwood spoons and the popular Excelle® 8-inch square cake pan with non-stick coating. Complete this apartment-warming gift with a plate of home baked Chocolate Mint Brownies, the ingredients for a quick and easy Tuna Pasta Casserole, and the recipes for both.

Tuna Pasta Casserole for Two

Excelle 8 in. Square Cake Pan

4 oz. pasta spirals, cooked
1 can (12¼ oz.) water packed
   tuna, drained and flaked
⅓ cup sliced water chestnuts,
   drained
⅓ cup sliced mushrooms
½ cup frozen peas
1 can (10 oz.) cream of
   mushroom soup
1 cup water or milk
½ teaspoon seasoned salt or
   to taste
¼ teaspoon garlic powder
⅛ teaspoon black pepper
1½ cups crushed potato chips
   (reserve 1 cup for topping)

Preheat oven to 350° F. Spray pan with non-stick cooking spray. In large bowl, combine all ingredients, reserving 1 cup of crushed chips for topping. Spread into prepared pan. Top with reserved crushed chips. Bake 20-25 minutes or until bubbly and chips are light golden brown.

Makes 2 servings.

Variation: Substitute canned French fried onions for potato chips.

Chocolate Mint Brownies

Excelle 8 in. Square Cake Pan

½ cup butter or margarine,
   softened
½ cup sugar
¼ cup packed brown sugar
2 oz. unsweetened baking
   chocolate, melted
1 egg, lightly beaten
½ teaspoon vanilla extract
¾ cup all-purpose flour
½ teaspoon baking soda
1 cup (6 oz.) mint chocolate chips
½-¾ cup Wilton Candy Melts®
   Dark Cocoa Mint (14 oz. pkg.)

*Brand confectionery coating

Preheat oven to 350° F. Grease pan with solid vegetable shortening or spray with non-stick cooking spray. In large mixing bowl, beat butter and sugars until smooth and creamy. Stir in melted chocolate, egg and vanilla. Mix flour and baking soda; add to creamed mixture. Stir. Add chips; stir. Spread batter into prepared pan. Bake 20-25 minutes or until toothpick inserted in center comes out clean. Place Candy Melts on brownies; let melt, then spread to frost brownies. Cool in pan on wire rack. Cut into 2 inch squares or diamonds.

Makes 16 brownies.

Half the fun of attending fall football games is the pregame tailgate feast. Your friends will cheer when you bring this hearty pasta, turkey and cheese salad made in our First and Ten Football Pan. Prepared in advance and well chilled, this salad should be transported in the pan in a cooler and then inverted just before serving. If you like, substitute deli ham or roast beef for the smoked turkey, and cheddar cheese for the mozzarella. Once you add this Football Pan to your kitchen collection, you'll find lots of occasions to use it... from birthday celebrations for boys of all ages to Super Bowl parties and sports banquets. Try it for baking bread loaves for meat and cheese hero sandwiches as well as traditional cakes.

Orzo and Smoked Turkey Salad

Wilton First and Ten Football Pan

Vinaigrette:

⅓ cup white balsamic vinegar OR white wine vinegar

1 tablespoon Dijon mustard

1½ teaspoons lemon juice

1 teaspoon salt

½ teaspoon dried oregano leaves, crushed

¼ teaspoon black pepper

⅔ cup olive oil

Salad:

1 package (16 oz.) orzo pasta, cooked, drained

1 tablespoon olive oil

½-¾ pound smoked turkey, cut into ¼-inch cubes PLUS thin slice turkey for garnish

8-10 ounces mozzarella cheese, cut into ¼-inch cubes

¼ cup coarsely chopped red pepper PLUS red pepper for garnish

2-3 tablespoons grated parmesan cheese

2 tablespoons chopped fresh basil OR 2 teaspoons dried basil leaves, crushed

½ teaspoon salt

¼ teaspoon black pepper

To prepare Vinaigrette: In small bowl, combine vinegar, Dijon mustard, lemon juice, salt, oregano and pepper. Slowly whisk in olive oil. Set aside. Spray pan with non-stick vegetable pan spray. Line with plastic wrap. In bottom of pan, make stripes of football with thin strips of turkey and lacing with red pepper.

To prepare Salad: In large bowl, coat orzo with olive oil. Add turkey, mozzarella cheese, red pepper, parmesan cheese, basil, salt and pepper. Stir in Vinaigrette. Pack mixture into prepared pan. Cover with plastic wrap. Refrigerate several hours or overnight. (It's best to prepare this salad one day in advance.) When ready to serve, invert onto serving tray.

Makes 8 servings.

Tired of bringing the same old bar cookies to every picnic? Then try this luscious fruit and cheese dessert. This sophisticated flavor combination of yellow cake, creamy blue cheese filling, and juicy grapes is a refreshing change of pace from gooey, rich desserts. Make it for summer picnics, backyard barbecues, and family reunions. It's prepared in the perfect pan for large quantity cooking—the Wilton 11x15 inch Covered Sheet Pan. This sturdy pan with cover makes it easy to tote foods to any large gathering.

Creamed Blue Cheese & Grape Dessert

Wilton 11x15-in. Sheet Pan with Cover

Cake Base:

4 eggs, separated
¾ cup granulated sugar, divided
3 tablespoons water
½ teaspoon vanilla extract
1 cup all-purpose flour
1¼ teaspoons baking powder
¼ teaspoon salt

Topping:

2 tablespoons plus ⅓ cup
   apple jelly, divided
2 packages (5.25 oz. each) Saga
   or blue cheese, crumbled
2 packages (8 oz. each)
   cream cheese
1 cup whipping cream, whipped
1½ lbs. red and green seedless
   grapes (approximately 6 cups)
½ cup coarsely chopped walnuts

Preheat oven to 425° F. Lightly grease pan.

To prepare Cake: In large bowl, beat egg whites until slightly mounded. Slowly beat in ½ cup sugar until mixture holds stiff peaks. In medium bowl, beat egg yolks, water and vanilla extract. Blend in remaining ¼ cup sugar. Combine flour, baking powder and salt; stir into egg yolk mixture until well mixed. Gently fold ¼ of beaten egg whites into egg yolk mixture. Then gently fold egg yolk mixture into stiffly beaten egg whites until well blended. Spread into prepared pan. Bake 12 to 15 minutes or until cake springs back when lightly touched and is lightly browned. Cool in pan on wire rack.

To prepare Topping: Microwave 2 tablespoons apple jelly in small microwavable dish on HIGH for 30 seconds or until melted. Cool 10 minutes. Combine crumbled blue cheese and cream cheese in microwavable bowl. Microwave on HIGH about 2 minutes or until soft but not melted; stir well to remove lumps. Stir in cooled melted apple jelly. Gently fold in whipped cream. Spread mixture evenly over cooled cake. Arrange grapes in decorative pattern over blue cheese mixture. Microwave remaining ⅓ cup apple jelly until melted: brush over grapes to glaze. Sprinkle with walnuts. Chill at least 2 hours before serving. See page 94 for tips on keeping take-along foods well chilled, fresh and safe.

Makes 24 servings.

When you're an overnight houseguest, a thoughtful gift for your host and hostess is this savory cream cheese, lox and onion cheesecake. It's a delicious spread for toasted bagels or English muffins. Prepare it one to two days in advance and chill before your visit. Then transport it to your destination right in the sturdy Wilton 9-inch Springform Pan inside your cooler. Even if everyone sleeps in, this convenient breakfast spread will be ready and waiting.

Savory Lox and Onion Cheesecake

Wilton 9-in. Springform Pan

Crust:
⅓ cup dry bread crumbs
¼ cup grated parmesan cheese

Filling:
1 medium onion, chopped
    (approximately ½ cup)
2 tablespoons chopped green onion
2 teaspoons butter
4 packages (8 oz. each) cream
    cheese, room temperature
4 eggs
½ cup heavy cream
½ lb. unsalted (Nova) lox,
    coarsely chopped
2 tablespoons grated parmesan
    cheese
½ teaspoon salt
¼ teaspoon black pepper

Preheat oven to 300° F. Spray pan with non-stick vegetable pan spray.

To prepare Crust: Sprinkle inside of pan with combined bread crumbs and parmesan cheese. Shake crumbs around sides and bottom of pan until well coated. Shake out excess crumbs.

To prepare Filling: Sauté both onions in butter until soft but not brown; set aside. Place cream cheese, eggs and cream in large bowl. Beat with electric mixer until blended and smooth. Stir in onions, lox, parmesan cheese, salt and pepper. Pour into prepared Springform Pan. Wrap bottom of pan with foil. Place Springform Pan in large baking pan; fill baking pan with hot water to depth of 1 inch. Bake 1 hour and 40 minutes. When done, turn oven off and leave cheesecake in oven 1 hour. Remove cake from water bath and place on rack to cool 30-60 minutes. Refrigerate overnight in Springform Pan. Remove from pan. Garnish with additional lox, green onions or chives, if desired.

Makes 12-20 servings.

This new twist on the traditional birthday cake is sure to appeal to men or anyone who prefers savory treats over sweet ones. Under cream cheese "icing" is a hearty sub sandwich in the round, built with whole wheat bread, popular deli meats, three kinds of cheese and flavorful spreads. It's best to assemble the "cake" a day in advance and "ice" it close to serving time. Use Wilton's 2-Piece Cake Saver to transport this super sandwich to the party. Before serving, pop open a package of Wilton Beer Can Candles. It's just one of many Wilton specialty candle sets that add fun and personality to any kind of cake.

Birthday Sandwich "Cake"

Wilton 8-inch Round Cake Pan, 3-in. Deep
Wilton Disposable Decorating Bags
Wilton Tip #21
Wilton Beer Can Candles
1 loaf (1 lb.) frozen whole wheat bread dough, thawed
¼ lb. each thinly sliced roast beef, turkey and ham
¼ lb. each thinly sliced provolone, Swiss and cheddar cheese
1 jar (6 oz.) roasted red peppers, drained
½ cup radish (or other) sprouts
4-5 large leaves leaf lettuce
Butter, softened
Horseradish to taste
Mayonnaise
Honey mustard
3 packages (8 oz. each) cream cheese, softened
Stuffed green olives

Spray pan with non stick vegetable pan spray. Form dough into 8-inch round loaf; press into pan. Cover and let rise 1-1½ hours or until doubled in bulk. Bake at 350° F for 20-25 minutes or until bread sounds hollow when tapped. Cool 5 minutes; remove from pan. Cool thoroughly. Cut horizontally into 4 equal slices. To assemble "cake": Line same pan with plastic wrap, letting enough wrap hang over sides to wrap bread. Spread bottom slice of bread with butter and horseradish; top with roast beef, provolone cheese and roasted red peppers. Spread second slice of bread with butter and horseradish and place it, butter/horseradish-side down, over roast beef layer. Spread top of this second bread slice with mayonnaise; top with turkey, Swiss cheese and sprouts. Spread third slice of bread with mayonnaise and place, mayonnaise-side down, over turkey layer. Spread top of this third bread slice with honey mustard; top with lettuce, ham and cheddar cheese. Spread cut side of loaf top (fourth slice) with honey mustard and place, mustard-side down, over ham layer. Place assembled "cake" in plastic wrap-lined pan and bring wrap up around "cake" to cover. Refrigerate 3-4 hours or overnight. (To make "cake" more compact and easier to ice, during refrigeration place a large pan over top of the 8-inch pan and weigh it down with heavy objects such as cans of food.) To ice "cake", beat cream cheese with electric mixer until light and fluffy. Remove "cake" from pan and place on serving board or bottom of Wilton 2-Piece Cake Saver. Spread top and sides of cake with cream cheese. Using tip 21, pipe cream cheese to make bottom shell border. Garnish with olives. Refrigerate until ready to serve. Top with Beer Can Candles.

Makes 6-8 servings.

Wrapping china, packing boxes, moving furniture ... what a way to work up an appetite! When your friends are in the midst of Moving Day, surprise them with a special lunch. These smoked sausage, onion and cheddar cheese bread loaves bake up crisp and golden brown in Wilton's perforated French Bread Pan.

The hearty loaves are delicious served at room temperature, making them convenient to serve whenever there's time for a break. Use a decorative wine gift bag to package your gift in style. Include some fresh fruit for nibbling and a bottle of wine for celebrating.

Sausage Filled Sandwich Loaves

Wilton French Bread Pan

2 loaves (16 oz. each) frozen Italian/pizza bread dough OR dough for 1½ -lb. loaf from bread machine (dough cycle)

10 oz. smoked sausage, cut into ¼-inch slices

1 medium onion, sliced

1 cup (4 oz.) shredded cheddar cheese

Thaw frozen bread dough according to package directions then bring to room temperature OR make dough in bread machine, setting machine to dough cycle. Remove dough from machine and divide in half. On a floured surface, roll each loaf (thawed dough) or half of dough from bread machine into approximately 4x8-inch rectangle. Cover and let rest 15 minutes. Meanwhile, sauté sausage in large skillet until browned; remove from skillet with slotted spoon or spatula. Add onion to same skillet; sauté until tender. Finish rolling dough into 8x12-inch rectangles. Spread half of sausage and onions on each rectangle; top with cheese. Roll up, pressing edges to seal. Heavily spray pan with non-stick vegetable pan spray. Place loaves in prepared pan. Cover and let rise in a warm place, about 1 hour or until doubled in size. Preheat oven to 350° F. Bake 30-35 minutes or until browned and bread sounds hollow when tapped. Cool 5 minutes and remove from pan. Cool completely before wrapping in plastic wrap. May be served at room temperature or reheated in oven.

Makes 6-8 servings.

PART III

HOLIDAY GIFTS

For celebrations and festive occasions, we offer a selection of special holiday recipes. Beautifully wrapped Christmas cookies and Valentine's Day candies are heartwarming gifts to make in your kitchen. When family and friends gather, help your hostess by bringing the dessert, dressed for the holiday. Starting in your kitchen, share all the warmth and love the holidays have to offer.

So much sweeter than the traditional card, these cookies and candies express love and affection straight from the heart. Our Valentine cookies are crisp and light with flavors of toasted almonds, cinnamon, and nutmeg. The dough is rolled, then cut with Wilton Heart Cookie Cutters. The Wilton Nesting Set gives you six popular sizes from which to choose. Tie an extra set to your gift basket for inexpensive decorative flair. The recipe for these brandy-soaked cherries with fondant and Candy Melts® makes enough for several gifts (with a few left for sampling, too). Package them in small containers in a bed of pink-tinted coconut. If you like, you can omit the chocolate heart shells and place cherries in Wilton Gold Foil Candy Cups. What a lovely way to say, "Be My Valentine!"

Almond Heart Cookies

Wilton 6-Piece Nesting Heart Cookie Cutter Set
Even-Bake Insulated Cookie Sheets
4 cups slivered almonds, toasted and ground
4 tablespoons all-purpose flour
2 teaspoons ground cinnamon
½ teaspoon ground nutmeg
3 tablespoons Wilton Meringue Powder
½ cup water
2 cups granulated sugar, divided
Confectioners sugar
Ground cinnamon
Wilton White Edible Glitter

In large bowl, stir together almonds, flour, cinnamon and nutmeg; set aside. In small mixer bowl, combine meringue powder, water and half of sugar. Beat at high speed 5 minutes. Gradually add remaining sugar and continue beating at high speed 5 minutes until meringue is stiff and dry. Fold into almond mixture. Cover and let stand 30 minutes so nuts will absorb mixture. (Dough needs to be firm enough to roll.) Preheat oven to 325° F. Spray cookie sheets with non-stick vegetable pan spray. On surface lightly sprinkled with confectioners sugar, roll dough to ¼-inch thickness. Dip cutters into confectioners sugar, cut cookies and place on prepared cookie sheet. Sprinkle cookies lightly with cinnamon and edible glitter. Bake 7-15 minutes, depending on size of cookie, or until lightly browned. Do not overbake. (Medium size cookies shown bake 10-12 minutes.) Cool on wire rack. Store cookies in airtight container.

Makes 2 dozen medium-size hearts.

Dipped Cherries in Chocolate Shells

Wilton Petite Heart Pan
Cherries
1 jar (16 oz.) maraschino cherries with stems
1 cup brandy
1 can (16 oz.) Wilton Candy Wafer and Fondant Mix
1 package (14 oz.) Wilton Candy Melts®*, Light or Dark Cocoa
Heart Shells
1 package (14 oz.) Wilton Candy Melts®*, Light or Dark Cocoa
1 package (14 oz.) Wilton Candy Melts®*, White
*brand confectionery coating

To make Cherries: Several days before making candy, drain juice from cherries in jar. Replace juice with brandy. Cover jar. Allow cherries to soak at least 24 hours or up to one week. Make fondant mix according to label directions for mints, OMITTING the mint flavoring. Drain cherries and place on paper towel Cherries should be dry before dipping in fondant. Dip cherries into fondant mixture. If mixture becomes too thick, thin with a small amount of water. Set cherries on waxed paper to dry. Melt candy according to package directions. Dip fondant covered cherries into melted candy, sealing candy to stem. Fondant and cherry must be completely covered to prevent cherries from leaking. Refrigerate to set. Cherries should be stored at cool room temperature.
To make Heart Shells: Prepare heart shells in Petite Heart Pan according to directions on Page 48 for Candy Pizzas. Melt white candy according to package directions; spoon into shells and top with cherry.

Makes 40-50 cherries.

This spring, bring our adorable lamb family to share Easter with your family. These easy to make cakes will delight adults and kids alike—they provide both a beautiful center-piece and a luscious dessert.

Buttercream icing piped in easy swirls gives the lambs their fleecy white coats. Charmingly detailed faces are made with Wilton Candy Melts®.

Easter Lambs

Wilton 2 Piece Stand-Up
   Lamb Pan Set
Wilton Mini Lamb Pan
Wilton Parchment Triangles
Wilton Candy Melts®*,
   Pink, Light Cocoa
Wilton Tips 4, 5, 16, 18
Wilton Rainbow Nonpareils
Wilton Leaf Green Icing Color

Baked cakes, prepared according
   to label directions on pans
Buttercream Icing (2 recipes)
Flaked coconut
Fresh flowers (optional)

*Brand confectionery coating

NOTE: For instructions on
specific decorating techniques,
see the current Wilton Yearbook
of Cake Decorating.

To prepare Candy Faces and Ears: Reserve 2 light cocoa wafers for garnish. Melt remaining Candy Melts® according to package directions, in separate containers. Place light cocoa melted candy in parchment bag with small opening cut at end. Pipe facial features on inside of pans. Chill 3-5 minutes. With pink melted candy, coat entire face area and ears, approximately ¼-inch thick. Chill about 15 minutes. Carefully unmold faces and ears onto clean kitchen towel. Set aside. Bake cakes according to label directions on pans; cool. **To prepare Stand-up Lamb:** Position cake on cake board, cut to fit. Using tip 5, outline legs with icing. Attach candy face and ears with icing. Using tip 18, cover lamb with icing in reverse shells for "wooly" effect. Sprinkle with nonpareils. **To prepare Mini Lambs:** For each lamb, attach two lamb halves together with icing. Using tip 4, outline legs with icing. Attach faces and ears with icing. Using tip 16, cover lamb with icing in reverse shells for "wooly" effect. Add light cocoa wafers, cut in half, for feet. Place coconut in plastic bag. Add a few drops icing color and shake until desired shade is achieved. Place lambs on serving platter. Sprinkle coconut around lambs on serving platter. Add fresh flowers, if desired.

Makes 16 servings.

Buttercream Icing

NOTE: You will need two recipes
for these lambs.

½ cup solid vegetable shortening
½ cup butter or margarine
1 teaspoon Wilton Clear Vanilla
4 cups sifted confectioners sugar
   (approximately 1 lb.)
2 tablespoons milk

Cream butter and shortening with electric mixer. Add vanilla. Gradually add sugar, one cup at a time, beating well on medium speed. Scrape sides and bottom of bowl often. When all sugar has been mixed in, icing will appear dry. Add milk and beat at medium speed until light and fluffy. Keep icing covered with a damp cloth until ready to use. For best results, keep icing bowl in refrigerator when not in use. Refrigerated in an airtight container, this icing can be stored 2 weeks. Rewhip before using.

Makes 3 cups.

When the Halloween spirits grab you, send ghostly greetings to friends and neighbors with these gifts from the kitchen. There's nothing scary about our happy Jack pumpkin muffins. Adults, especially, will enjoy these richly-spiced muffins for a wholesome Halloween breakfast. Arrange the muffins in a handsome basket for gift giving. Surprise little ghosts and goblins with pretzels in clever disguise. The trick to making both Halloween treats is to cook with quality Wilton bakeware and Wilton confectionery ingredients.

Pumpkin Muffins

Wilton Mini Pumpkin Pan
1¼ cups all-purpose flour
½ cup whole wheat flour
1½ cups sugar
1 teaspoon baking soda
¼ teaspoon salt
1 teaspoon ground cinnamon
½ teaspoon ground nutmeg
½ cup oil
⅓ cup water
2 eggs
1 cup canned mashed pumpkin
½ cup chopped walnuts

Heat oven to 350° F. Spray pan with non stick vegetable pan spray. In large bowl, combine flour, whole wheat flour, sugar, baking soda, salt, cinnamon and nutmeg; mix well. In medium bowl, combine oil, water, eggs and pumpkin; mix well. Add pumpkin mixture to flour mixture and beat 1 minute at medium speed on electric mixer. Fold in walnuts. Pour batter into prepared pan, filling ¾ full. Bake 25-30 minutes. Cool 5 minutes. Remove from pan. Serve warm or cool to room temperature.

Makes 6 muffins.

Halloween Pretzels

Wilton Candy Melts®*
    White, Orange, Green
    and Light Cocoa
    (14 oz. packages)
Wilton 9 in. Pie Pans
Wilton Tips #2, 3, 352
Wilton Pumpkins Icing
    Decorations
Wilton Parchment Triangles
Pretzel rods
Chewy chocolate-flavored
    candy rolls

*brand confectionery coating

Melt candy in separate containers according to package directions. Pour orange and white melted candy into separate pie pans. Roll pretzels in melted candy to coat, place on waxed paper; let set. With small spatula, add additional melted candy to pretzels for a textured look. **To make Pumpkins:** Using melted light cocoa candy in parchment triangles and tip 2, pipe facial features. Using melted green candy and tip 352, add leaves to top. Roll candy roll on table to make smaller in diameter; cut into ½-inch pieces. Attach stem to top. **To make Ghosts:** Using white melted candy and tip 3 in parchment triangles, pipe arms. Attach pumpkin icing decorations. Using melted green and light cocoa candy and tip 2, pipe facial features. Let set. Stand pretzels in basket of candy corn.

Many of us can't help but overindulge at the Thanksgiving table. Luckily this pumpkin chiffon dessert is a deliciously light alternative to traditional pumpkin pie. Spiced with cinnamon and nutmeg, the golden pumpkin filling is spooned into a nut pastry crust made in the Wilton 10-inch Springform Pan. The pumpkin mixture is prepared with Wilton Meringue Powder which eliminates the need to use raw egg whites. Still, this dessert should be well chilled before packing it in your cooler to take to the family feast. Special for children are these cinnamon-sugar turkey cutouts. Reminiscent of the days of helping mom in the kitchen, our flaky crust recipe allows for making plenty of Thanksgiving cinnamon-sugar pastries. Gobble! Gobble!

Pumpkin Chiffon Pie & Turkey Treats

Wilton 10-in.
    Springform Pan
Wilton Perimeter Turkey
    Cookie Cutter
Wilton Cookie Sheet

Nut Crust:

2¼ cups all-purpose flour
1 cup finely chopped walnuts
    or pecans
2 tablespoons
    granulated sugar
½ cup cold butter (1 stick)
4-6 tablespoons cold water
Ground cinnamon
Granulated sugar

Filling:

2 packages unflavored gelatin
1 cup cold water, divided
1 can (16 oz.) pumpkin
1 cup granulated
    sugar, divided
½ cup packed brown sugar
¼ cup brandy
1½ teaspoons ground
    cinnamon
¼ teaspoon ground nutmeg
2 tablespoons Wilton
    Meringue Powder
1 cup whipping cream,
    whipped OR 2 cups frozen
    whipped topping, thawed

To prepare Crust and Cookies: Preheat oven to 375° F. Combine flour, nuts and 2 tablespoons sugar in large bowl or work bowl of food processor fitted with steel blade. Cut butter into flour mixture with pastry blender or on/off pulses of food processor until mixture resembles coarse crumbs. Add water, a few tablespoons at a time, until dough just holds together. Divide dough into two parts, ⅔ and ⅓. Form into flat disks and refrigerate at least 30 minutes. On lightly floured surface, roll larger disk to 14-inch circle. Fold into quarters and place in pan. Unfold dough and press onto bottom and 2 inches up sides of pan. Do not stretch dough. Prick bottom of crust with fork. Roll second disk to ¼ inch thickness and cut with floured turkey cutter. Sprinkle turkeys with cinnamon and sugar. Place on ungreased cookie sheet. Bake crust 25-30 minutes, cookies 10-15 minutes. Cool crust before filling.

To prepare Filling: Sprinkle gelatin over ½ cup cold water in medium saucepan; let stand 5 minutes to soften. Add pumpkin, brown sugar, ¼ cup granulated sugar, brandy, cinnamon and numeg; stir over medium heat until very hot. Set aside to cool. In large bowl, beat meringue powder, remaining ½ cup cold water and ¼ cup granulated sugar on high 2 minutes. Add remaining sugar and continue beating until stiff peaks form, about 3 minutes. If pumpkin mixture is not cool, stir over a bowl of ice water until cooled. Add 1 cup of meringue to pumpkin mixture; stir. Gently fold pumpkin mixture and whipped cream into remaining meringue. Pour into cooled crust. Chill at least 3-4 hours or overnight. Garnish with additional whipped cream or whipped topping and nuts, if desired.

Makes 8-10 pie servings, 8-10 turkey cookies.

Hanukkah, the Jewish Festival of Lights, is a time for happy family celebration. Special gingerbread and sugar cookies are enjoyed in many Jewish families during the eight days of Hanukkah. For children, bake up these fragrant gingerbread Star of David cookies sprinkled with blue-colored  sugar. Package them in a simple tin that later can be used for storing crayons and markers. Present adults with beautifully symbolic sugar cookies and sugar cubes decorated with dreidel, menorah and Star of David designs in traditional blue and white Hanukkah colors.

Hanukkah Gingerbread Stars

Wilton Cookie Sheet or Pan
Wilton 6 Point Star Cookie Cutter
Wilton Royal Blue Icing Color
¼ cup Granulated Sugar
Gingerbread Cookie Recipe (p. 35)

Preheat oven to 375° F. In small bowl, tint sugar with icing color until desired color is reached. Prepare cookie dough according to directions up to pressing in pan. On floured surface roll out dough ¼ inch thick. Cut dough with lightly floured star cutter. Place on ungreased cookie sheet. Sprinkle stars with colored sugar. Bake 8-10 minutes or until lightly browned at edges. Let cool on sheet 2-3 minutes. Remove carefully with large spatula. Cool completely on wire rack. Store in a loosely covered container in a cool dry place.

Makes 2-3 dozen cookies.

Variation: Omit colored sugar; decorate cookies with royal icing (p. 35) or poured fondant.

Hanukkah Color Flow Cookies

Wilton Round Nesting Cookie
   Cutter Set
Wilton Tips 2, 3, 14
Wilton Royal Blue, Golden Yellow,
   Red-Red Icing Colors
Wilton Cookie Sheet
Sunflower Sugar Cookie
   Recipe (p. 80)
Hanukkah Design Patterns (p. 96)
Cookie Icing:
1 cup sifted confectioners sugar
2 tsps. milk
2 tsps. light corn syrup
Color Flow Icing:
(Full-Strength for Outlining)
¼ cup water + 1 teaspoon
1 lb. sifted confectioners sugar (4 cups)
2 Tablespoons Wilton Color Flow
   Icing Mix

Preheat oven to 400° F. Prepare Sunflower Cookie Dough Recipe, omitting chocolate chips. Divide dough into 2 balls. On a floured surface, roll each ball into a circle approximately 12 inches in diameter and ⅛ in. thick. Cut cookies, dipping cutters in flour before each use. Bake on middle rack of oven for 6-10 minutes, or until cookies are lightly browned. Cool 5 minutes on cookie sheet. Carefully remove cookies with spatula to cooling rack. Allow to cool completely before decorating.

For Cookie Icing, place sugar and milk in bowl. Stir until mixed thoroughly. Add corn syrup and mix well. To ice cookies, place on rack with drip pan below and pour icing over cookies. Let dry. After icing has "crusted over" lightly trace desired patterns with toothpick.

For Color Flow Icing: In an electric mixer, using grease-free utensils, blend all ingredients on low speed for 5 minutes. If using hand mixer, use high speed. Color Flow Icing "crusts" quickly, so keep it covered with a damp cloth while using. Stir in desired color. To fill in an outlined area, this recipe must be thinned with ¼ teaspoon of water per ¼ cup of icing. Outline patterns on cookies in full-strength color flow with tip 2. Thin color flow and fill in design. Pipe scrolls and dots in full-strength color flow with tip 3; stars with tip 14.

Makes 2-3 dozen.

Sugar Cubes

Wilton Tips 1, 1s
Wilton Royal Blue, Golden Yellow,
   Red-Red Icing Colors
Sugar cubes
Royal Icing Recipe (p. 35)

Trace patterns on sugar cubes with toothpicks. Outline patterns in royal icing with tips 1 and 1s.

Note: Icing dries hard—sugar cubes are perfect to serve for use in hot beverages.

'Tis the season for thinking of others. When families gather for a cozy Christmas brunch, help the hostess by bringing this yuletide breakfast entree—cheesy scrambled eggs in a home baked bread loaf. The bread is easy to make with convenience frozen dough. Wilton's Treeliteful pan gives the loaf its festive shape. Surprisingly, this dish can be completely assembled and refrigerated the night before. Simply reheat in the morning. For that special butcher, baker, candlestick maker or other professional you adore, make these fancy career cookie ornaments. With the wide variety of Wilton Cookie Cutters available, you'll find an appropriate design for every person on your list. Use your imagination to create one-of-a-kind Christmas tree decorations.

Christmas Tree Breakfast Bread

Wilton Treeliteful Pan
2 loaves (1 lb. each) frozen
    bread dough, thawed
1 egg plus 2 tablespoons
    water for glaze
¼ cup butter, divided
1 medium onion, chopped
18 eggs, beaten
¼ cup milk
1 teaspoon salt
¼ teaspoon black pepper
1 can (4 oz.) chopped
    green chilies, drained
1 can (2¼ oz.) sliced pitted
    ripe olives, drained
1 jar (7¼ oz.) roasted red
    peppers, drained
1 cup (4 oz.) shredded
    Monterey Jack cheese

Let dough come to room temperature. Reserve approximately 2 inches dough from end of one loaf for decoration. On lightly floured surface, knead remaining dough together then roll into a triangle about 8 inches on each side. Cover and let rest 15 minutes. Spray pan with non-stick vegetable pan spray. Roll and press dough to fit pan. Brush lightly with water. Form reserved dough into garlands and ball for top of tree; lay on top of loaf. Cover and let rise in warm place 1-1½ hours or until doubled in bulk. Preheat oven to 350°F. Brush loaf with egg glaze. Bake 25 minutes or until loaf sounds hollow when tapped. Remove from pan; cool. Split loaf and remove bread to make ¾-1 inch shell. Brush inside shells with 2 tablespoons melted butter. Place on cookie sheet, cut surfaces up, and return to oven 15 minutes to toast. Cool. Melt remaining 2 tablespoons butter in large non-stick skillet. Sauté onions until tender. Add combined eggs, milk, salt and pepper to skillet. Cook over medium low heat until almost set, stirring occasionally. Add chilies, olives and ½ cup chopped roasted red peppers. Continue to cook eggs until dry. (These eggs are best when cooked until dry, not soft.) Cool. Spoon eggs into bottom bread shell; sprinkle with cheese. Add top of bread shell; wrap with foil. If serving immediately, heat in 350° F oven 5 minutes. If refrigerated overnight, reheat foil-wrapped filled loaf in 350° F oven 25-30 minutes or until thoroughly heated. Garnish with remaining roasted red pepper, cheddar cheese, Monterey Jack cheese and chives.

Makes 8-10 servings.

Career Cookie Ornaments

**Wilton Apple, Boy, Train
    Perimeter Cookie Cutters**
Wilton Tips 1, 2, 3, 13
**Wilton Golden Yellow, Kelly
    Green, Royal Blue, Black,
    Brown, Christmas Red,
    Copper Icing Colors**
Wilton Parchment Triangles
Gingerbread Cookie Recipe (p. 35)
Color Flow Recipe (p. 72)
Royal Icing Recipe (p. 35)

Preheat oven to 375°F. Prepare Gingerbread Cookie Dough per directions. Roll out on a lightly floured surface to 1/8 in. thick. Cut cookies, dipping selected cutter into flour before each use. Using the small open end of tip 3, cut hole in cookie for hang cord. Bake on ungreased cookie sheet for 8-10 minutes, until lightly browned at edges. Remove with spatula and let cool completely on wire rack before decorating. NOTE: If you're not going to use your gingerbread dough right away, wrap it in plastic and refrigerate. Refrigerated dough will keep for a week, but be sure to remove it 3 hours prior to rolling so it softens and is workable. Bake dough not needed for ornaments to make delicious Christmas cookies.

For decorating instructions, see Inside Back Cover.

For Stevie From Aunt Zella

❧ CHRISTMAS COOKIE DUO ❧

Come December, there are dozens of times for eating and for sharing Christmas cookies. Fortunately, baking them is also a most enjoyable holiday tradition. These two cookies aren't fragile, making them good choices for taking to cookie exchanges, office gatherings and holiday open houses. Better yet, they are excellent choices for mailing—enabling you to send edible Christmas wishes to out-of-state relatives and friends. (See pgs. 94-95 for more about mailing gifts of food.) The Fruit Chews are chock-full of dried fruits, nuts, and coconut. Red and green Wilton Candy Melts add a festive note, as do the cheery Santa & Elves Mini Baking Cups. The irresistible, buttery shortbread trees are simple, pat-in-the-pan cookies made in the Wilton Petite Christmas Tree Pan.

Fruit Chews

Excelle Mini Muffin Pan
Wilton Santa and Elves Mini
  Baking Cups
1 package (6 oz.) diced mixed
  dried fruit
1 cup chopped walnuts
1 cup flaked coconut
¾ cup graham cracker crumbs
½ cup packed brown sugar
2 eggs
1 teaspoon vanilla extract
36 Wilton Christmas Mix
  Candy Melts® (optional)*

*Brand confectionery coating

Preheat oven to 350° F. Line pan with baking cups. Combine fruit, walnuts, coconut, graham cracker crumbs, brown sugar, eggs and vanilla. Fill each cup with a scant tablespoon of mixture. Press into cups. Bake 10-12 minutes or until set and lightly browned around edges. Remove to wire rack. While still hot, top each with a Candy Melt, if desired. Let sit 5 minutes; spread to ice. Continue to cool. Repeat with remaining mixture.

Makes approximately 36 cookies.

Shortbread Trees

Wilton Petite Christmas
  Tree Pan
Wilton Icing Colors
  (optional)
Wilton Green and Red
  Crystal Sprinkle
  Decorations
1 cup butter, softened
¾ cup sugar
1 teaspoon vanilla
2½ cups flour
Confectioners sugar (optional)

In medium mixing bowl, cream butter, sugar and vanilla. Add flour and mix until dough is smooth. If colored dough is desired, add icing color and mix. Chill dough 1 hour. Preheat oven to 300° F. Spray pan lightly with non-stick vegetable pan spray. Press dough into prepared pan cavities, to ⅛-inch from top of pan. Top with sprinkle decorations, if desired. Bake 12-18 minutes or until very lightly browned. Cool 10 minutes in pan on wire rack; remove shortbread to complete cooling. Sprinkle with confectioners sugar, if desired. Shortbread can be stored in an airtight container at room temperature for several weeks or frozen for up to two months.

Makes 4 dozen cookies.

✦ PART IV ✦

GIFTS *for* CHILDREN

*Imaginative and fun best describe our
chapter for children. Here are gifts to
give to kids and gifts for kids to give.
We feature recipes that will encourage
children to think of others—cheerful
flowerpot cookies for grandparents and
a peanut butter teddy bear cake
for a favorite babysitter. We have
gift ideas to get children started cooking
and some recipes that are just plain fun,
because being a kid should be.*

Whatever the season, these sunny sunflowers always brighten the day! Our tasty cookies are fun for children to make and give, for any occasion or no occasion at all. They're baked on lollipop stick stems and planted in grassy beds of green tinted coconut in new clay pots. Available in dozens of shapes and sizes, Wilton Cookie Cutters are perfect for creative baking and crafts. Let your children make modeling clay gifts with our simple directions for charming photo frames and napkin rings. Clay art is just one of many uses you'll find for our imaginative cutter collection—they're great for everything from place cards to party sandwiches.

Sunflower Cookies

Wilton Flower
    Perimeter Cookie Cutter
Wilton Cookie Sheets
Wilton Lemon Yellow
    Icing Color
Wilton 8 in. Lollipop Sticks

1 cup butter or
    margarine, softened
1 cup sugar
1 large egg
1 teaspoon vanilla
2 teaspoons baking powder
3 cups all-purpose flour, divided
1 cup semi-sweet chocolate chips

Preheat oven to 400° F. In a large bowl, cream butter and sugar with an electric mixer. Beat in egg and vanilla. Add baking powder and 2 cups of the flour, 1 cup at a time, mixing well after each addition. Tint dough with icing color. Stir in remaining 1 cup flour by hand. (Dough will be very stiff.) Do not chill dough. Pinch off small amount of dough; make twelve to eighteen ¼-inch balls. Place balls, 3 inches apart, on ungreased cookie sheets. Each ball will be used as a base to support sunflower cookie on stick. Press lollipop stick into dough; set aside. Divide remaining dough into 2 balls. On a floured surface, roll each ball into a circle approximately 12 inches in diameter and ¼ inch thick. Cut dough, dipping flower cutters in flour before each use. Place cookie over stick and press lightly. Add chocolate chips for center. Bake on middle rack of oven 6 to 10 minutes, or until cookies are lightly browned. Cool 5 minutes on cookie sheet. Carefully remove cookies with spatula to cooling rack. Allow to cool completely before picking up by sticks.

Makes 12-18 cookies.

To make Flower Pots: Cut styrofoam to fit into small clean clay pots. Tie bow to lollipop stick then secure stick in clay pot. Cover styrofoam with green tinted coconut.

Variation: Omit lollipop sticks and flower pots. Bake cookies as directed.

Cookie Cutter Crafts

Wilton 6-Piece Nesting Heart
    Cookie Cutter Set
2 oz. yellow modeling compound
2 oz. blue modeling compound
(Use the type of compound which is
    hardened in the oven.)

For Picture Frame: Cut two hearts the same size with heart cookie cutter. For front of frame, cut center out of one heart with a smaller heart cookie cutter. Use other size heart cutters to imprint outline on frame. Bake pieces separately according to clay package instructions. When cool, glue photo to back. Glue front to back over photo. For a hanging frame, place ribbon loop between front and back before gluing.
For Napkin Rings: Roll out compound to ¼-inch thickness. Cut strips 5½x½-inch. Form strips into circles, overlapping ends and pressing together. Bake on sheet as shown. Cut hearts, making extra for flower pots, if desired. Bake according to clay package instructions. Glue hearts to rings and pots when cool.

Makes 1 frame, 4 napkin rings and 3 hearts for flower pots.

Distance often prevents us from attending special birthday celebrations. But this crispy cereal cake is a delightful way to send greetings across the miles to young friends. The marshmallow-coated rice cereal mixture is pressed into Wilton's Dalmatian Pan then turned out and decorated with melted cocoa candy.

A fast, easy birthday message is spelled out with Wilton Icing Decorations. Be sure to enclose candles and mail according to our handy directions on page 95. You can make crispy cereal cakes in all sorts of shapes using Wilton Novelty Pans. These snack cakes are fun to send to kids at camp and even to students away at college.

Crispy Cereal Puppy

Wilton Dalmatian Pan
Wilton Tip 4
Wilton Disposable Decorating
　Bags
Wilton Alphabet Icing
　Decorations

Body:
½ cup margarine plus margarine
　to prepare pan
8 cups miniature marshmallows
12 cups crisp rice cereal
½ package Wilton Candy Melts®*,
　Light Cocoa

Ears:
2 tablespoons margarine
3 cups miniature marshmallows
3 cups chocolate flavored crisp
　rice cereal

*brand confectionery coating

Grease pan with margarine. Prepare body and ear mixtures separately. Melt margarine in large saucepan; add marshmallows. Cook and stir until melted. Add cereal and mix well. Place cereal mixture for body in pan; add chocolate cereal mixture for ears. Press the two mixtures together. Invert. Reserve 2 Candy Melts. Melt remaining candy according to package directions. Using tip 4, outline legs, paws, mouth and nose. Use reserved Candy Melts for eyes. Add icing decorations and ribbon for bow. Let cool completely before packaging for mailing. See page 95 for tips on how to mail.

Makes 16 servings.

Birthdays, bake sales and classroom parties...with kids, there's always a need for special school treats. Look to Wilton for clever food ideas the whole class will love. Math lessons will never be the same after these gumdrop cakes come to class. They're baked in Wilton's Numbers Pan Set, then simply packaged with plastic wrap and ribbon. Just get ready to count the compliments. Miniature snacks are appealing to children and the perfect size for small appetites. These petite chocolate brownies are baked up chewy in Wilton's Muffin Munchies Pan then sandwiched together with a creamy icing. Decorate them with Wilton Icing Decorations in holiday or famous character designs to match the occasion or party theme. Wrap in plastic wrap and tie with ribbon. Then sell them individually or by the dozen at the next school fund raiser.

Gumdrop Number Cakes

Wilton Numbers Pan Set
1⅓ cups sugar
4 eggs
1 cup butter or margarine, melted
⅔ cup milk
1 teaspoon vanilla extract
2⅔ cups flour
2 teaspoons baking powder
Small gumdrops

Preheat oven to 350° F. Grease and flour pans. (**Do not** use non-stick vegetable pan spray.) In medium bowl, beat sugar and eggs lightly. Beat in butter, milk and vanilla extract. Add flour and baking powder, mixing until batter is smooth. Arrange gumdrops, flat-side down, in decorative pattern in bottom of pans. Carefully spoon batter over gumdrops. Bake 20-25 minutes or until toothpick inserted in center comes out clean. Cool 5 minutes in pan; invert onto wire rack. Cool.

Makes 9 cakes.

Easy Brownie Sandwiches

Wilton Muffin Munchies Pan
Wilton Icing Decorations
2 large eggs
1 cup sugar
½ cup butter or margarine
2 ounces unsweetened chocolate
¾ cup all-purpose flour
½ teaspoon salt
1 teaspoon vanilla
Buttercream Icing recipe (Page 66)

Preheat oven to 325° F. Spray pan with non-stick vegetable pan spray. In medium mixing bowl, beat eggs; blend in sugar. Melt butter and chocolate in heavy saucepan over low heat or in microwave in microwavable bowl on MEDIUM. Stir into egg and sugar mixture. Add remaining ingredients and stir (do not beat) until well mixed. Pour batter into prepared pan. Bake 10-15 minutes or until toothpick comes out clean. Do not over bake. Cool in pan on wire rack; remove and cool. Sandwich tops together with buttercream icing. Attach icing decorations with additional icing.

Makes approximately 3 dozen.

The next time you need a gift for a youngster, skip the toy store and head to the kitchen. This sweet gift is perfect for preschoolers on a birthday, at Christmas, or just for a surprise. Start by making a simple sugar-cookie dough in chocolate and vanilla flavors, form into rolls and refrigerate. Use ribbon to attach adorable bite size Wilton Cookie Cutters to an apron for their very own. (Be sure to slip the cookie recipe into the apron pocket for Mom.) It's easy for children to slice the cookie dough, then cut with cookie cutters. The cut out shapes get mixed and matched to make two-flavor cookies. They can be served with a glass of milk at snacktime or with lemonade at the next tea party.

Vanilla & Chocolate Refrigerator Cookies

Wilton Bite Size Bear &
Elephant Perimeter
Cookie Cutters
Wilton Cookie Sheet
1 cup butter, softened
1 cup granulated sugar
2 eggs
1½ teaspoons vanilla
2¾ cups all-purpose flour
½ teaspoon baking soda
½ teaspoon salt
1 square (1 oz.) unsweetened
chocolate, melted

In large bowl, cream butter with sugar. Add eggs, one at a time, beating after each addition. Add vanilla and mix well. Stir in dry ingredients. Divide dough in half. Stir melted chocolate into one half. Shape dough into rolls, 2¼-inches in diameter. Wrap in plastic wrap and chill until firm, 3-4 hours or overnight. Preheat oven to 400°F. Using half vanilla and half chocolate, slice the dough into ¼-inch slices. Place on ungreased cookie sheet. Using bear and elephant cutters dipped in flour, cut half of each flavor of the sliced dough into bears and half into elephants. Place vanilla bears into chocolate bear cut outs and chocolate into vanilla. Repeat with elephants. Bake 8-10 minutes or until light golden brown.

Makes approximately 2 dozen.

With a little adult help, your child will love baking this bear and brightening a babysitter's, teacher's or grandparent's day. It's a scrumptious cake, featuring the favorite flavors of peanut butter, jelly and chocolate. Wilton Dark Cocoa

Candy Melts® and string licorice are used for Teddy's charming features. The Wilton Huggable Bear Pan is lined with foil so once baked and cooled, the cake can easily be lifted from the pan and wrapped—ready for giving.

Babysitter's PB&J Cake

Wilton Huggable Bear Pan
Wilton Candy Melts®*,
    Dark Cocoa (14 oz. bag)

Topping:
1 cup all-purpose flour
½ cup firmly packed brown sugar
½ cup butter
1 cup chocolate chips

Cake:
1 cup firmly packed brown sugar
½ cup peanut butter
½ cup butter, softened
4 eggs
1 teaspoon vanilla
2 cups flour
½ teaspoon baking powder
½ cup chocolate chips
½ cup almond brickle chips
½ cup strawberry or grape jam
Red string licorice

*Brand confectionery coating

Preheat oven to 350° F. Line pan with foil that extends over edges of pan. Spray foil with non-stick vegetable pan spray.

To prepare Topping: In small bowl, combine flour and brown sugar. With pastry blender, cut in butter until mixture resembles fine crumbs. Stir in chocolate chips, set aside.

To prepare Cake: In large bowl, beat brown sugar, peanut butter, butter, eggs and vanilla until light and creamy. Beat in flour and baking powder until smooth. Stir in chocolate and almond brickle chips. Pour batter into prepared pan. Bake 20 minutes. Spread strawberry jam over cake. Sprinkle with reserved Topping. Use Candy Melts to decorate bear. Cut 1 melt in half and place in each ear. Use 1 melt for paws, nose and each eye. Cut licorice for mouth and criss-cross designs on body. Bake an additional 25-30 minutes or until jam starts to bubble through topping, or until cake tested with toothpick comes out clean. Cool thoroughly on wire rack before lifting cake from pan.

Makes 12 servings.

Here's a neat gift idea for a young person learning to cook. To assemble this gift, start by preparing the dough for these Chocolate Chunk Cookies. Next, drop the dough onto cookie sheets with Wilton's Cookie Scoop, then freeze. Once the dough is frozen, package the cookie "scoops" in a freezer-safe container.

Label the container with baking directions and it's ready to give. Complete this gift for your aspiring young chef with some essential cookie-making equipment—a Wilton Cookie Scoop, the Even-Bake Insulated Cookie Sheet (perfect for uniform baking with no burning) and a Wilton cooling grid. Include some favorite cookie recipes, especially this yummy one.

Chocolate Chunk Cookies

Even-Bake Insulated
Cookie Sheet
Wilton Cookie Scoop
2½ cups old fashioned or quick oats, uncooked
2 cups flour
1 teaspoon baking powder
1 teaspoon baking soda
½ teaspoon salt
1 cup unsalted butter, softened
1 cup granulated sugar
1 cup packed brown sugar
2 eggs
1 teaspoon vanilla
12 ounces semi-sweet or milk chocolate, coarsely chopped
1½ cups coarsely chopped walnuts

Place small amount of oats in blender container; process until powdered. Repeat until all oats are powdered. Combine powdered oats, flour, baking powder, baking soda and salt; mix well. In large bowl, beat butter and sugars with electric mixer until light and fluffy. Blend in eggs and vanilla. Add dry ingredients to sugar mixture; mix well. Stir in chocolate and walnuts. Chill at least 1 hour. Preheat oven to 375° F. Dip cookie dough with cookie scoop; place 2 inches apart on ungreased cookie sheet. Bake 10-12 minutes or until lightly browned. Remove cookies to wire rack to cool.

Makes about 4 dozen.

Freeze Ahead Directions: Prepare cookie dough as directed above. Using cookie scoop, drop balls of dough, close together, onto ungreased cookie sheet. Freeze. Place frozen dough in airtight container. When ready to bake, preheat oven to 375° F. Place frozen cookie dough, 2 inches apart, on ungreased cookie sheet. Bake 15-20 minutes or until lightly browned.

What a day for a picnic! We've planned an imaginative lunch kids will love, perfect for taking on your next trip to the zoo. Sandwiches cut with Wilton Animal Cookie Cutters, fruit salad served in animal print baking cups, and inside out cupcakes with Wilton Jungle Animal Icing Decoraions add up to ferocious fun! And all of these foods are safe to tote in your picnic basket. When you're not visiting the animals, serve these friendly foods at the park or on the patio. Surprise your children, a niece, or a nephew with a gift of your time and fun foods from your kitchen.

Zoo Sandwiches

**Wilton Bear and Elephant
   Perimeter Cookie Cutters**
Raisin bread
Whole wheat bread
Cream cheese, softened
*Shredded carrot or
   raisins (optional)*
Butter, softened
Cheddar cheese slices
Pimento for garnish

Cut bear shapes from raisin bread slices and elephant shapes from whole wheat bread slices. Spread bear shaped bread slices with cream cheese; fill sandwiches with carrots or raisins, if desired. Spread elephant shaped bread slices with butter (or your child's favorite spread). Fill sandwiches with cheese. Attach garnish (cheese blanket and eye, pimento dots, raisin eyes) with small amount of butter. Pipe Bear bow using cream cheese inside a disposable decorating bag fitted with tip #2. Wrap sandwiches in plastic wrap or place in airtight container.

Fruit Salad

**Wilton Jungle Animals
   Standard Baking Cups**
Wilton Standard Muffin Pan
**Wilton Jungle Animals
   Icing Decorations**
½ honeydew melon, peeled and seeded
½ cantaloupe, peeled and seeded
1 apple, cored
1 pear, cored

Cut all fruit into small chunks. Place baking cups in muffin pan and fill with fruit. Overwrap with plastic wrap or place in snug fitting plastic bag. Refrigerate until ready to pack for picnic. When ready to serve, add icing decoration to top of fruit.

Makes 8 servings.

Inside Out Cupcakes

Wilton Muffin Caps Pan
**Wilton Jungle Animals
   Icing Decorations**
*1 package (9 oz.) yellow cake mix
   (1 layer size)*
*1 cup chocolate icing, homemade
   or purchased*

Preheat oven to 350°F. Spray pan with non-stick vegetable pan spray. Prepare cake mix according to package directions. Spoon 3 tablespoons batter into each cavity, filling almost to top. Bake 12-15 minutes or until lightly browned. Cool 5 minutes; remove from pan and cool completely on wire rack. For each cupcake, sandwich two cakes together with 2 table-spoons icing. Attach icing decoration with small amount of chocolate icing. Wrap individually in plastic wrap.

Makes 7-8 cupcakes.

GIFT TIPS

We hope our recipes have inspired you to make many homemade gifts from your kitchen to share with friends and family. As you've discovered, there are all kinds of foods and all types of occasions for gift giving.

✣ WRAPPING IT UP ✣

Attractive and appropriate packaging of your gift is important. After all, foods that look good seem to taste even better. If you have a spare shelf in a pantry, closet, or basement, keep a supply of food packaging containers and wrappings on hand.

Baskets, boxes, tins, jars, and gift bags are all useful food containers. New clay or ceramic flower pots are quite clever. You can recycle plastic food containers or coffee cans. Plastic produce baskets, woven with ribon, lace, rickrack, or raffia, are adorable and inexpensive holders. Fancy paper plates or food storage bags tied with decorative ribbon are perfect for a selection of home baked cookies. For kids, buy a new sand pail or lunch box to package your gifts.

Cooks, both new and seasoned, will enjoy a gift of food packaged in new Wilton Bakeware—bowls, baking pans, even cookie sheets. Bread boards and chopping boards are great for holding wrapped loaves of quick bread.

Get into the habit of buying gift containers and wrapping supplies when you happen upon them so you'll have a ready supply for your gifts from the kitchen. You can always find decorative plates and

platters at department and housewares stores. But for containers that are inexpensive and just as pretty, visit craft and party shops, or grocery and discount stores. Even drug and hardware stores are a source. There are many interesting items at antique stores, thrift shops, and garage sales that make good containers. Housewares stores specializing in import items have many unique and reasonably-priced objects for food gifts. Try to shop the after holiday sales for the best bargains.

Once you've selected a container, personalize it, if you like. Use pretty napkins or fabric to line baskets or boxes. Fabric is easier to handle than paper gift wrap and is available in seasonal themes and unique patterns. A circle of fabric cut with pinking shears can be tied around the lid to dress up jars. Paper ribbon, raffia, lace, and cords add decorative touches to your gifts. Cotton printed ribbons tie nicely around any size or shape package. Keep a selection of Wilton Doilies on hand. They're available in white, gold, and silver and are pretty liners on plates and platters of irresistible cookies and candies.

Clear or colored cellophane is useful for enclosing gifts of food contained in pans, bowls, or large baskets. Tie-ons add the finishing touch to your package. Experiment with party favors, fresh or dried flowers and herbs, cinnamon sticks, candy canes, lollipops, or a set of Wilton Cookie Cutters or Wood Spoons, to name just a few.

Finally, "go-along with" gifts make special accompaniments. Include a bottle of fine wine with fancy hors d'oeuvres, micro-brewery beers with casual appetizers, a wedge of imported cheese with a savory bread loaf, gourmet coffees with cake, or flavored teas with dainty cookies.

✣ ON THE PRACTICAL SIDE ✣

When you give a gift of food, be sure to label it. After all, people like to know what it is they're eating. Your label should contain any storing or reheating from years past, cut to size, note cards, or recipe cards for beautiful gift tags and labels. Many cooks also like to include the recipe with their gift.

Handle gifts of food with care. Always use food-safe materials, such as plastic wrap or foil, for wrapping gifts of food. Baked goods to be wrapped should be thoroughly cooled first or moisture will collect under the wrapping. If your gift is a baked casserole or hot dish meant to be enjoyed that night, call ahead to let the recipient know it's coming and to arrange a convenient time for delivery. If your container isn't a disposable one or cookware meant to be a gift, label it with your name on masking tape on the bottom, to ensure you get it back.

✢ CARRYING CAUTIONS ✢

The old rule still applies: keep cold foods cold and hot foods hot. Be especially careful with foods that contain eggs, cream, mayonnaise, poultry and meat.

If you're giving cold foods as gifts or taking them to picnics or outdoor events, keep them cold while transporting. Remember to chill cold foods thoroughly or even freeze, if appropriate, before carrying them in an insulated cooler with ice packs. If your item is too large for a cooler, pack ice packs around the container, then wrap in many layers of newspapers.

To carry hot foods, tuck a length of fabric, cloth napkins or a kitchen towel around the food container and place in a sturdy box or pan just larger than the food container. Fabric insulates and is pretty draped around your food container. Newspaper is also a good choice to keep the heat in.

To carry cakes, the Wilton Cake Saver is the answer—it's great for standard size cakes, desserts and pies. For other cakes, use Wilton Cake Boards, available in many sizes. Cut the boards to the shape of your cake, dessert, or bread and wrap them with Wilton colored foil or contact paper. Place cake in a sturdy box.

✢ MAILING TIPS ✢

To mail cakes successfully, start by choosing a very dense cake, such as pound or chocolate (page 14), or a crispy cereal cake (page 82).

Cakes baked in covered pans are perfect for sending and make a nice "two gifts in one" gift. Be sure to tape the lid to the pan with masking tape. Then pack in a carton close to the same size as the pan. Place packing materials around the pan so it won't shift during handling. For cakes not in covered pans, first secure cake to cake board with a generous amount of Buttercream Icing (page 66). The cake board should be about the same size as the cake and the shipping box should be about the same size as the cake board. Be sure to select a sturdy box about an inch higher than the cake. Secure the cake board on the bottom of the box with doublestick tape. Reinforce corners of the box with styrofoam, so the top flaps can't be pushed in on top of the cake. Do not add any packing material or covering around or over the cake. To send breads, cool thoroughly, then wrap in plastic wrap or foil. For cookies, choose fairly moist, sturdy cookies or bar cookies. Wrap cooled cookies individually or in pairs, back to back, in plastic wrap. Pack breads and cookies in bubble wrap, styrofoam pellets, or unseasoned, unbuttered popcorn. Bar cookies can be baked and sent right in their pan—our Covered Jelly Roll or 9x13 Cake Pans are popular choices—in a sturdy shipping box. Two day or priority mail is always a good idea for packages containing food.

Instructions For Christmas Cookies, p.74

For Color Flow Icing: Use full-strength Color Flow icing and tip 2 or 3 to outline with desired colors. If using the same color icing to fill in the outlines, let outlines dry a few minutes until they crust. If filling in with icing that differs in color from the outlines, then let outlines dry thoroughly (1-2 hours) before filling in. To fill in an outlined area, recipe must be thinned with ½ teaspoon of water per ½cup of icing.

For Royal Icing: Beat all ingredients at low speed for 7 to 10 minutes (10 to 12 minutes at high speed for portable mixer) until icing forms peaks.

Decorate Cookies as Follows:

Wilton Decorator—Use Royal Icing. Using tip 2, outline and pipe-in lt. copper face and hands; white apron; black pants; yellow shirt; white shoes with black outlines. Pat down with finger dipped in cornstarch. Add tip 2 brown swirled string hair; dot blue eyes and lt. copper nose; red string mouth and lt. copper ears. Add tip 1 black string shoelaces and blue message on apron.

Apple—Use Color Flow Icing and tip 2. Outline, then flow-in red for fruit, green leaf, brown stem. When set, add green veins on leaf and black message.

Train—Use Color Flow and Royal Icings. Using Color Flow, add tip 3 black outlines to wheels, flow in white centers. Use Royal Icing for the following: Add tip 3 red engine outlines, star fill in using tip 13. Pipe in grey smoke stack; pipe-in black window, add lines above engine and smoke stack. Add black cowcatcher and brake shaft.

Police Officer—Use Royal Icing. Using tip 3, outline and pipe in lt. copper face and hands; blue cap, pants and shirt; black belt, shoes and visor. Smooth with finger dipped in cornstarch. Add yellow hair, blue dot eyes, lt. copper dot nose and string ears, red string mouth. Pipe in blue collar, black tie, grey badge.

When icing is dry, thread gold cord through hole on cookies for hanging. Address cards and attach to cookies with dots of icing.

Note:
For specific decorating techniques, see the current Wilton Yearbook of cake decorating.

✢ CREDITS ✢

Creative Director	Richard Tracy
Food Editor	Zella Junkin
Recipe Development	Lois Levine
	Donna Land
Food Stylists and Decorators	Lois Hlavak
	Andrea Duggan
	Patty Higgins
	Susan Matusiak
	Steve Rocco
	Mary Gavenda
	Corky Kagay
Photography	Kathy Sanders
Photo Assistant	Cristin Nestor
	Kathy Ores
Copy Editor	Jeff Shankman
Writer	Sharon Riskin
Production Coordinator	Mary Stahulak

Wilton Products used in this book are available from your local Wilton deal You can also write or call:

Wilton Enterprises
Caller Service #1604
2240 W. 75th St., Woodridge, IL 60517
1-708-963-7100

Copyright 1995 Wilton Enterprises. All rights reserved. No part of this publication may be reproduced o transmitted in any form, or by any means, electronic or mechanical, including photocopy, recording or information storage and retrieval system, without the written permission of:

Wilton Enterprises, 2240 W. 75th St., Woodridge, IL 60517. A Wilton Industries Company

Printed in U.S.A

Hanukkah Cookie Patterns, p.73